Third
Wheel

BY COMMON CONSENT PRESS is a non-profit publisher dedicated to producing affordable, high-quality books that help define and shape the Latter-day Saint experience. BCC Press publishes books that address all aspects of Mormon life. Our mission includes finding manuscripts that will contribute to the lives of thoughtful Latter-day Saints, mentoring authors and nurturing projects to completion, and distributing important books to the Mormon audience at the lowest possible cost.

Third Wheel

Peculiar Stories of Mormon Women in Love

Melissa Leilani Larson

For information contact
By Common Consent Press
4062 S. Evelyn Dr.
Salt Lake City, UT 84124-2250

The purchase of this book, while deeply appreciated, does not grant the purchaser performance rights. Applications for permission for any use must be made in advance and a license to perform obtained from the author before rehearsals begin.

If you are interested in producing this play at any level—amateur, academic, or professional—please contact the author at leilani.prods@icloud.com.

Cover design: D. Christian Harrison; illustration by Emily Call
Book design: Andrew Heiss

www.bccpress.org

ISBN-10: 0-9986052-3-9
ISBN-13: 978-0-9986052-3-4

10 9 8 7 6 5 4 3 2 1

Contents

Acknowledgments

Thanks to Dare Clubb, whose one-act assignment would lead me to *Little Happy Secrets*. I'm also grateful to my classmate Morgan Sheehan, whose nuanced reading of Claire on an April afternoon helped me realize I had created something special.

Thanks to Jerry Rapier and Cheryl Cluff for including me in the Plan-B Lab; that invitation, coupled with a bout of bronchitis, led to the first draft of *Pilot Program*.

Thanks to the friends whose feedback helped shape these pieces, particularly Shelley T. Graham, Janine Sobeck Knighton, James Goldberg, Jessica Dart, Bianca Morrison Dillard, Jenn Chandler, Landon Wheeler, Dave Mortensen, Heather Bodie, Elizabeth Leavitt, Amanda Schutz, and Phillip Clayton.

Many thanks to the talented actors, directors, and designers with whom I've been privileged to work. Because of you, these plays have become inhabited worlds.

I've been blessed by the example of great teachers: Eric Samuelsen, Barta Heiner, Elizabeth Hansen, Art Borreca, and Sherry Kramer. Thank you.

Thanks to my family for their patience when it comes to this hobby I refuse to let be a hobby.

Finally, thanks to Melanie Hess for being my person, no matter what, and to Ben Hess for letting us get away with it.

Melissa Leilani Larson:
playwright

Melissa Leilani Larson is a problem solver. For years, in addition to writing some of the smartest, wisest plays I know, she worked as a theater stage manager. Stage managers, in case you're not familiar with theatrical nomenclature, are the staff sergeants of the theater world. Directors decide what approach any production will take, what a show's overarching concept will be, how the show will look, move, feel, what it will mean. Stage managers make it happen. Directors work closely with the actors to create their characterizations, help them work out how they will interpret their lines, how their movement in space will realize an overall stage picture. Stage managers make sure the actors show up on time, memorized and ready to work. Directors work with designers, conceptualizing a set, lighting, sound. Stage managers make sure the set gets built, on time, under budget, and that it's safe to walk on.

But it's more than that. Mel did work on shows with big casts and budgets. But she also worked in smaller, local theaters, with tiny budgets and unpaid, volunteer labor. She's great at working with limited resources, of making do, improvising, getting a show on its feet by sheer force of will. And she was legendary for her unflappable temperament, her resolute humor in difficult circumstances, her mild but formidable omnicompetence. A Mel Larson show worked. It came together.

Her problem-solving skills also served her well in her work as a playwright/adapter. In my opinion, her stage adaptations of Jane Austen's novels are nonpareil. And what is a Jane Austen adaptation but an exercise in problem-solving? Those marvelous novels, with complex stories, with many fascinating characters (especially minor characters, who are among Austen's richest creations), pose the most demanding trials for the playwright. How to condense so enchanting a story to a couple of hours entertainment? What do you cut; what do you keep? How do you tell a complicated tale simply enough so it can be understood, using Austen's rather dense (to our ears) language, while still retaining the charm and wit and incisive social commentary of the originals? How do you balance the three Jane Austens: the satirist and comic, the unquenchable romantic, and also the fiercely committed feminist? Nobody does it better than Mel Larson, in part because she is also those three things: satirist, sympathetic romantic, and feminist.

But now, in the plays in this collection, we see another side of Larson's work. In these plays, she explores, with wit, insight and compassion, the toughest issues of her own culture. And what gives these plays their unique texture and power is our dawning recognition that these are issues without a solution. Mel Larson, the problem solver and pragmatist, faces problems that can't be solved. Not neatly, and not easily, at least.

Austen's protagonists are women, and they include some of the most richly textured characters in literature: Elinor Dashwood, Anne Elliot, Elizabeth Bennet. They are, all of them, middle-class British women, more or less comfortably situated in their own oh-so-British culture. For her own stage creations, Mel writes women that are every bit the equal of Austen's heroines. They're Mormons; women who are deeply and personally committed to the Church of Jesus Christ of Latter-day Saints. Comfortably located in their cultures too, at least initially. Claire, in *Little Happy Secrets*, has fallen in love. Or maybe not; maybe she's just enthralled, in the grips of a deep romantic attraction. But she's a committed member of the LDS faith, and she's in love with another woman. And Abigail, in *Pilot Program*, has agreed to share her husband with another woman, as, she believes, is required of her by her Church leaders. And Abigail loves her husband deeply, and, scarred by her own battles with infertility, thinks another wife might provide him with the child she knows he wants. Both women are in love. Both women find, in and through their love, torment and agony. And things are unlikely to change for them, or improve.

And we know both women very well indeed, in part because they talk to us. While *Little Happy Secrets* is largely about the relationship between Claire and Brennan, the central relationship of the play may be between Claire and the audience. This is also likely true of Abigail, who blogs to us.

Both plays could be called tragedies. But both defy easy definitions. Mel writes with wit and affection about her own culture, and both plays have moments of humor. Above all, though, the plays lead to conversation. After seeing them, we audience members seem compelled to talk about them. The test of a great play isn't whether audiences laugh, or cry. It's the degree to which the play gets under your skin. After seeing either play in a good production, you can't let it go. You talk in the car on the way home. You wake in the middle of the night, thinking about it.

Again, it's about problem-solving. My wife and her sisters do this all the time. When we get together, they raise an issue they're facing. Perhaps a child faces a personal dilemma; how to help her resolve it? I'm in a dispute with a neighbor; what should I say, and when? Informal conversations about the challenges of LDS life, about reconciling the occasional tensions of life, from a Christian/Mormon perspective take place, I think, all the time in LDS culture. Wasn't it Joseph Smith who wrote "by proving contraries, truth is made manifest?" And so, in our finest contemporary playwright, we have a woman whose best work proves (tries, tests?) the contraries of our culture. She's a pragmatist, a practical woman. Deeply committed to her own understanding of what we call the Restoration, but acutely in tune with the difficult paradoxes of gender and sexuality and patriarchy embedded within Mormon culture. She poses problems that can't be solved and leads us toward the pain and heartache that results. These plays have been produced, and with distinction. They need to be produced again and again. We deserve these conversations.

—Eric Samuelsen

Little
Happy
Secrets

a play
by Melissa Leilani Larson

In memory of Hollie Beard, who, I like to think, would enjoy being in this play.

And for Courtney Jensen. Because she is a rock star.

When the evening was over, Anne could not be amused. . . nor could she help fearing, on more serious reflection, that, like many other great moralists and preachers, she had been eloquent on a point in which her own conduct would ill bear examination.
—Jane Austen, *Persuasion*

Little Happy Secrets premiered at the New Play Project in Provo, Utah from March 19–23, 2009, with the following cast:

Claire	Laurel Sandberg-Armstrong
Brennan	Christie Clark
Carter	Jake Welch
Natalie	Maggie Laurencell

Directed by Landon Wheeler. Costumes by Jennifer Jenkins, lighting by Eric Johnson, and dramaturgy by James Goldberg.

Settings

Various locations in and around Provo, Utah in 2007–08. There are also brief scenes in Seattle, Portland, and Mesa.

The set should be minimal, as the scenes are short and changes happen quickly, driven by narration and light.

Characters (3 W, 1 M)

CLAIRE, mid-20s   BRENNAN, mid-20s

CARTER, mid-20s   NATALIE, early 20s

Production notes

One of the most important aspects to be considered is intimacy, as Claire frequently addresses the audience. This is a memory play, its events presented through the filter of Claire's recollection. For this reason certain moments in the play should be stylized to an extent: e.g., the kiss should be implied rather than actually performed.

All of the characters are practicing Latter-day Saints (Mormons), which should be taken into account in regard to costume and behavior.

Sometimes silence is everything.

A set of ellipsis points (. . .) indicates a brief pause, perhaps a hesitation, especially at the beginning of a line. A double set (. . . . . .) indicates a significantly longer pause.

Lights on CLAIRE.

CLAIRE   If I were to tell you where it began . . . I don't think I could, actually. I don't think I could put a mark on it as easy as that. Maybe I could . . . Sorry, I can be a little indecisive at times. If I were to put a mark on it, if I were to declare to the world, "This is the point, this is the genesis, the beginning of everything," you know, pointing with one of those foam finger things you get at football games in states where football matters more than life itself, then I would say it was the day Bren moved into Sky House. We hadn't seen each other in almost two years, since I went on my mission and she went on hers, and we had plotted to live together when we both came back to school. Who knew that seeing her again—seeing her so tan and healthy after eighteen months in the Australian sunshine—would hit me the way it did. It literally took my breath away. That's a phrase people use all the time, and you wonder where it comes from, what it means, until it happens to you. Until it happens, and just like that your lungs have sharp edges and it hurts to inhale or exhale, and your throat constricts like you're choking but there's nothing to choke on. It all happens in a split second, when you shudder a little in your step and take a moment to blink back to reality. Nope, you're still alive; your heart didn't really burst just now.

BRENNAN   Omigosh, Claire?

CLAIRE   Bren! Wow— This is like—

Aubrey Reynolds as Brennan, Jessica Myer as Claire. Echo Theatre. © 2013 Jaron Hermansen.

BRENNAN   It's been ages.

CLAIRE   Literally.

BRENNAN   How was Hamburg?

CLAIRE   Hahm-burg. Long "a." Pretend there's an "h" in there, too. It was great, Germany was great.

BRENNAN   I suppose I know that, I mean, from your letters, of course. Your letters were so great. I haven't been the best about that.

CLAIRE   Just made me thrill a little more when a letter did come. I've missed you.

Freeze frame. Right there, this is it. This is it. Brennan, standing on the stoop, our stoop, holding A&E's *Pride and Prejudice* five-volume set, with a box on the walkway next to her containing the complete works of Colin Firth. This is the moment— God, why does it hurt like this? Nothing should hurt like this, like open heart surgery, but you shouldn't know what that feels like, to get your ribcage cracked open, because you're under, unconscious on a metal slab. This, this moment should be good, glorious, but I feel like my chest is going to explode when she says—

BRENNAN I've missed you, too.

CLAIRE You look really good.

BRENNAN Stop it.

CLAIRE No, really, amazing.

BRENNAN I love it in Perth, it's gorgeous. I'm saving up to go back.

CLAIRE You just got home.

BRENNAN What can I say? I fell in love. You'll have to come visit.

CLAIRE You're moving to Australia.

BRENNAN It was a joke, Claire. I didn't mean it.

CLAIRE . . . Right, sorry, a joke, my bad.

BRENNAN I just had the best eighteen months of my life, is all.

CLAIRE Really? The best?

BRENNAN Wasn't it for you?

CLAIRE I don't know. I guess.

BRENNAN The house is in better shape than I expected.

CLAIRE   Yeah, Heidi and company took good care of it.

BRENNAN   Where is Heidi?

CLAIRE   Graduating. Elementary education. Plus she's getting married in November.

BRENNAN   November? Who wants to get married in November? "Happy Thanksgiving, and welcome to our receiving line?" No time at all for a honeymoon.

CLAIRE   She's done with school but he's got something like three years left. They're going to do the honeymoon thing at Christmas.

BRENNAN   That sucks. Why not put off the wedding till Christmas so you can do it right? You're just going to run out of time over Thanksgiving.

CLAIRE   I don't know.

BRENNAN   They just want to do it. It's ridiculous. I swear, people get married for all the wrong reasons.

CLAIRE   Not all people.

BRENNAN   Well, fine, but most of them. Don't you remember— What is her name? Our Ukrainian roommate sophomore year.

CLAIRE   Sonya.

BRENNAN   Is that right?

CLAIRE   *(overlapping)* Yeah, yeah, it is—

BRENNAN   *(overlapping)* Uh, no. No, that's not right. Are you sure?

CLAIRE　Yes. She was a convert and her name was Sonya—

BRENNAN　Okay, fine, it was Sonya. The point is, do you remember that weekend that she and her fiancé drove up to Wendover, got married, did it, and then got the marriage annulled?

CLAIRE　They did not.

BRENNAN　I'm telling you, it's true. And they didn't even stay together after that. She ended up marrying someone else. I mean, that's a lot of trouble for an orgasm, don't you think?

CLAIRE　Bren is always good at talking about things you just shouldn't talk about. Not good in the sense of tact; she'll just talk about it anyway.

BRENNAN　Are you ever tempted to do that?

CLAIRE　What?

BRENNAN　Have a flash wedding. Just to do it.

CLAIRE　No.

BRENNAN　Stop being so good. Of course you've thought about it.

CLAIRE　I'm not good. There are plenty of things that I—think about.

BRENNAN　Like?

CLAIRE　I look at her for a minute. I could tell her now. I could tell her why my mission had seemed eternal, why I felt a tremendous guilt teaching when my mind was elsewhere. My heart—

I kind of want the room in the back, but I'll let you pick.

I should follow, I should cover, I should try to make it look like nothing's wrong. But I sit on the step and let a wave wash over me. Relief? Regret? Why am I being so melodramatic?

Let me tell you something about Mormons. Latter-day Saints if you prefer. I prefer. We are tremendously good at looking like we're keeping secrets. Keeping things on the lowdown. We're so good at it that when the secret comes out, it's almost like a sin's been committed, like something dreadful has happened, even if the secret is innocent. That's what we do, that's why people think we're weird. "Peculiar," as Brigham Young said. People assume we have something to hide, they always have. Sure, there are the sacred things, the things that get spat upon by those who don't care enough to understand. But there's a difference between sacred and secret.

What secrets there are, we keep them from each other. How we're doing, what we're doing. It's like if something happens, you don't want the ward to find out. But then you have friends and neighbors and roommates, and everyone whispers to everyone else, and everyone guesses. That's the worst, when everyone guesses, because then everything gets blown out of proportion, and sometimes you have to spill the beans just to stop people talking. But no one stops talking. They can't, because everyone knows there's a secret. They treat it with care, sure, though that doesn't stop them from telling each other: "They broke up," and "He came home from his mission early," and "She's bulimic." You don't want everyone in the ward to know the ins and outs of your life, so you try to keep them to yourself. It's not like everyone's completely gossip crazy. It's more of a concern thing, you know? The ward, the congregation, it's like your extended family. Especially when you're away at school. So naturally, everyone worries about everyone else. Though sometimes you can't help wishing that people would keep their worrying to themselves. Maybe we actually suck at keeping secrets.

BRENNAN   You won't believe what happened today.

CLAIRE   What?

BRENNAN   I was going to my College Democrats meeting in the Kimball Tower.

CLAIRE   FYI: there are exactly six card-carrying members of the Brigham Young University chapter of the College Democrats of America. And two of those cards belong to Bren, because she lost her first one.

What do you people do at those meetings, anyway, other than judge Republicans?

BRENNAN   We're on season four, okay? When Sam runs for Congress.

CLAIRE   You are truly a model for a better tomorrow.

BRENNAN   You're hilarious. Why can't a person go anywhere in this state and proudly declare themselves a Democrat?

CLAIRE   Because people would glare at you like you're a fallen woman, all the while praying for your lost soul.

BRENNAN   The Church isn't Republican. The leadership, the General Authorities, they're politically neutral.

CLAIRE   As they should be.

BRENNAN   That doesn't mean I can't be a Democrat.

CLAIRE   Then be a Democrat.

BRENNAN   This is the U.S. of A., right? I can voice my opinions, I can say what's on my mind.

CLAIRE   Here we go.

BRENNAN   Things are wrong around here, with all these conservatives running loose—

CLAIRE   Conservatives don't run; they drive.

BRENNAN   SUVs the size of Texas with terrible gas mileage that cost more to maintain than a third world country.

CLAIRE   And expensive cars are an exclusively Republican transgression.

BRENNAN   Around here just about anything is an exclusively Republican transgression.

CLAIRE   You don't have any solid political logic backing this, do you? You're a liberal because it's the

Laurel Sandberg-Armstrong as Claire, Christie Clark as Brennan. New Play Project.
© 2009 Jen Jenkins.

minority. You just want to be the only one. Once you graduate and leave you'll switch parties like that.

BRENNAN   Will not.

CLAIRE   Then why, dare I ask, are you a liberal?

BRENNAN   It looks better on paper. The word.

CLAIRE   The word—?

BRENNAN   Yeah. "Liberal." Shorter, rounder sounds. Love that it starts and ends with an "l."

CLAIRE   That's completely inane.

BRENNAN   It is not.

CLAIRE   That's the most ridiculous reason for political staunchness I've ever heard. And here I am thinking you're a Democrat because Rob Lowe is hot.

BRENNAN   So I like *The West Wing*. It's idealist, so what?

CLAIRE   You know, he's a Republican on *Brothers & Sisters*.

BRENNAN   What are you talking about?

CLAIRE   The TV show, *Brothers & Sisters*. Rob Lowe is a Republican with a gay brother.

BRENNAN   . . . Whatever. What I'm saying is, I don't want to get lumped in with the spoiled little rich kids whose parents let them take new BMWs to school freshman year. Have you seen the parking lot outside of Heritage Halls? BMW, Lexus—

CLAIRE   You mean "Lexi." Isn't that the proper plural?

BRENNAN   You're the English major, you tell me.

CLAIRE   Are you going to lecture me on abortion now?

BRENNAN   I was hoping we would start somewhere smaller, like homeland security or illegal immigration.

CLAIRE   Right, yes, smaller. Excellent. What happened?

BRENNAN   Sorry?

CLAIRE   You were on your way to watch *West Wing* season four with the other heathen Democrats when—

BRENNAN   I missed the meeting.

CLAIRE   I think the earth just stopped moving. Oh, wait— There, it's going again.

BRENNAN   I met someone.

CLAIRE   Okay, so this is one of those key moments when things that could go so well just kind of— don't. I mean, we were only three weeks into fall semester, but we had fallen into old patterns. We had lunch together almost every day; we had a goal to meet at home and make something, to save money, which worked for a while. Sunday was quiet: church and meetings and drives up the canyon with the windows rolled down. Tuesday was fifty-cent night at the dollar movie and Wednesday we went grocery shopping and watched bad TV. Friday nights were set aside to show appreciation for Ben and Jerry and movies we had already seen way too many times, because who was actually going to ask us out?

BRENNAN   His name is Carter.

CLAIRE   Correction: Who was actually going to ask me out?

BRENNAN   We just stood there in the Quad, talking. I mean, he literally ran into me. How cliché is that?

CARTER   Whoa, hey, sorry. Are you—?

BRENNAN   It's all right—

CARTER   I wasn't really paying attention. I mean—

BRENNAN   Don't worry about it.

CARTER   Brennan, right?

BRENNAN　. . . Yeah. How did you—

CARTER　It was a long time ago, but do you remember Tracey—

BRENNAN　Tracey Bird. Yes. You were at that—

CARTER　Yeah.

BRENNAN　Oh, wow. That was a while ago. Good memory.

CLAIRE　I can see them, standing together at the southwest corner of the Quad, near the old library and the JKB, with the fall sun setting and a slight breeze. They're smiling at each other like something out of a Nora Ephron movie—a regular Tom Hanks/Meg Ryan moment—and I think I might throw up. I don't know what they talked about; I wasn't there, of course. But I can imagine.

CARTER　You've never been? You totally need to go. The salsa is amazing.

BRENNAN　I'm not so good with the Mexican.

CARTER　You'll love it. We could— Why don't I take you?

BRENNAN　. . . Sure, that'd be great.

CLAIRE　Sometimes I wish my imagination was a little less active.

BRENNAN　So we're going to dinner.

CLAIRE　Oh, hell. At least, that's what I thought; I didn't say it out loud.

Dinner? When?

BRENNAN   Friday.

CLAIRE   And you said yes? Just like that.

BRENNAN   Yeah. Isn't it crazy?

CLAIRE   That's one word for it. You don't even know him.

BRENNAN   We've met before. And I'll get to know him.

CLAIRE   Can't you be a normal returned missionary? Can't you think awkward thoughts about the opposite sex while experiencing feelings of inadequacy and invisibility?

BRENNAN   What are you, fourteen? I'm not going to marry him, it's just dinner. And it's Mexican, so who knows how it's going to go.

CLAIRE   It went well. They did Italian two nights later, and Brazilian two nights after that. And then Bren came home for lunch less and less and it was like . . .

BRENNAN   Hi.

CLAIRE   . . . Hi.

BRENNAN   Something wrong?

CLAIRE   No, nothing. I just— I haven't seen you in a while.

BRENNAN   It's been like two days.

CLAIRE   Still.

BRENNAN   Sorry, I've been busy.

CLAIRE   And she's off to class. No other explanation except for "Sorry, I've been busy." I'm in school too, you know. Who isn't busy? Nowadays fifth graders are booked morning to night. I deserve a better explanation than that: "I've been busy." We have history, we have a rapport, we have—

BRENNAN   Can I borrow your black skirt?

CLAIRE   Sorry?

BRENNAN   You know, the shiny one that's almost too short.

CLAIRE   Um...

BRENNAN   Carter and I are going to see this show and I want to look really good.

CLAIRE   You always look really good.

BRENNAN   Sorry, what?

CLAIRE   ... It's in the closet, on the right.

BRENNAN   Thanks.

CLAIRE   I'm feeling gutsy, because I'm feeling pouty, and feeling pouty strangely makes me feel gutsy. So I follow her into my room and watch her go through my closet. And Gutsy Me speaks up before the tried and true Thoughtful Me can get a word in.

So . . . Carter, huh? You've been seeing a lot of him lately.

BRENNAN   We've got a lot to talk about.

CLAIRE   Really.

BRENNAN   What's that supposed to mean?

CLAIRE   I just wonder. I haven't even met him. Besides, anyway, it's like I never see you because you're always off with Carter.

BRENNAN   That's not true.

CLAIRE   When was the last time you came home for lunch?

BRENNAN   I don't know, a couple of days?

CLAIRE   Seventeen days.

BRENNAN   You're kidding. Wait, you know that off the top of your head?

CLAIRE   We just—we haven't—you and I—

BRENNAN   Sorry, this is Carter, I've been trying to reach him all afternoon.

CLAIRE   Whoever invented the cell phone should get drawn and quartered. Truly. Instead of continuing what I wanted to be an intense and important conversation, she takes Carter's call, about whatever he finds so very earth-shatteringly important.

CARTER   I've got two words that are going to put a smile on your face: Cold Stone.

CLAIRE   And she's gone. So I wait. The thing is, whenever he called, whenever Carter called, Bren didn't come back. It's another three days before . . .

Someone's had a good day.

BRENNAN   Yeah, well . . .

CLAIRE   Carter?

BRENNAN   Maybe.

CLAIRE   Good grief.

BRENNAN   I'm happy, Claire. Be happy for me.

CLAIRE   I'm trying, I promise.

> I promise, I promise. She's holding my hand, Father. She's holding my hand, and there's a current running from her palm into mine, tiny little electrodes giving off tiny little waves of energy. Waves that continue to ripple even after she lets go. Heavenly Father, I . . . Sometimes I wonder why I need to say these things out loud when Thou hearest my thoughts before I think them. I know, I know, this is the principle of prayer, there is a point to regular, sincere, vocal communication with Thee. I know that, but it feels like I'm doing this wrong. It feels like I'm doing everything wrong. I just— I— Steel my heart. Please. If I'm feeling what it is that I think I'm feeling, then something is going to get broken, and I'd really rather it wasn't.

BRENNAN   Carter's coming over, and he's bringing a friend.

CLAIRE   Oh, joy. I can't pick up my cup, what with all the running over.

BRENNAN   His name is Truman.

CLAIRE   What is it with you and former presidents?

BRENNAN　You need to go out, you need to socialize. And Truman is getting an M.A. in English. He's going to be a poet.

CLAIRE　Yippee-ki-yay for him.

BRENNAN　Honestly, you could be an adult about this. You might already know him.

CLAIRE　There are hundreds of people in the English department. It's massive. I don't even know all the faculty, let alone any of the grad students.

BRENNAN　I thought you wanted to meet Carter.

CLAIRE　I do, of course I do. Just not on a double date. Maybe another time?

She doesn't roll her eyes at me, she just glares, that look she gets when she doesn't have the slightest clue what's going on in my head and really doesn't have the desire to find out because she knows it will just annoy her. But she accepts the rain check, and the following week we go out to lunch, the three of us. Former President Truman does not make an appearance, and I'm all right with that.

CARTER　So, Claire. Brennan tells me you're an English major.

CLAIRE　Is he trying to sound like my Uncle Mitch?

Yep. And you're pre-law.

CARTER　Yep.

CLAIRE　This is where we insert what some like to call a pregnant pause.

. . . . . . I'm sitting across the table from Brennan and Carter in Burgers Supreme, waiting for the people behind the counter to call out order 256. He's handsome enough, I guess. Carter. Extremely clean cut. Very expensively dressed; everything on him down to his key chain has a top-tier brand attached to it. It's possible he shops the outlets, but I doubt it. On this particular day he's wearing a pink button-down Oxford. It takes a certain man to wear a pink shirt. Not everyone can pull it off, except maybe Hugh Grant or Ralph Fiennes. Bren does have a liking for Colin Firth. Carter doesn't have the British thing going for him, but I have to admit he looks good. Thing is, he doesn't hold a candle to Bren. She just—lights everything up. And, like those sad, little insects that fly into flames only to burst and pop, I can't turn away.

CARTER   256, they said 256.

CLAIRE   Sorry?

CARTER   That's you, isn't it? 256?

CLAIRE   Oh, right. Sure.

It wasn't his fault that I hated him from the moment I met him. I mean, he seemed like a perfectly nice person who looked good in his starched pink Van Heusen and happened to know my order number better than I did.

CARTER   . . . So.

CLAIRE   So.

Jessica Myer as Claire, Aubrey Reynolds as Brennan, Kevin O'Keefe as Carter. Echo Theatre. © 2013 Jaron Hermansen.

Napkins are fascinating things when conversation is at an all-time low.

BRENNAN   Carter has an appreciation for Jane Austen.

CLAIRE   Really.

CARTER   Uh, sure.

CLAIRE   Which is your favorite?

CARTER   Um, I kind of like the one with Keira Knightley, but the Gwyneth Paltrow one is pretty funny. You know, "Try not to kill my dogs . . . " That's pretty great.

CLAIRE   You're kidding. Have you actually read any of her books?

BRENNAN   Claire.

CARTER   No. I guess it's the movies I like. I had to read *Pride and Prejudice* for a class but it got really dry, so I rented the—

CLAIRE   Dry? You found *Pride and Prejudice* to be dry?

CARTER   257, that's us. Be right back.

BRENNAN   What is wrong with you?

CLAIRE   An appreciation for Jane Austen is an appreciation for the wit and the power of her language, not for two-bit film adaptations.

BRENNAN   You're being such a snob. You love those movies.

CLAIRE   It's because I've read the books, I know the books. You can't see the movies and declare a passion for Jane Austen.

BRENNAN   Why not?

CLAIRE   Because he doesn't know you as well as I know you.

Okay, that was apparently completely the wrong thing to say. Of course I felt bad about it, I had huge guilt. If I'm the *Titanic*, then guilt is my iceberg. Yes, I'm overstating. Exaggerating. I do read a lot of novels, if you couldn't tell. And Carter—though I was all too ready to compare him to a rake like Willoughby or Wickham, the truth is I got used to Carter over time. I grew a tolerance for him, like blisters from new shoes turn into calluses. Being around him all the time, it made me—tougher. At first, listening to the two of them talk, being on the outside of some invisible barrier, my throat would clench and my eyes brim. Not like that feeling ever went away; I just got really good at hiding it. The funny part was Carter. He seemed to enjoy the fact that he and I were in this weird brother/sister/ love/hate thing, like he sensed the competition between us and dug in rather than give up. He started to call me about the most random stuff.

CARTER   Hey, Claire, I just got *Thundercats* on DVD if you want to watch it.

CLAIRE   *Thundercats*? Really? My favorite show when I was six . . . I'd actually enjoy that.

CARTER   Does Brennan like Cafe Rio?

CLAIRE   Who doesn't like Cafe Rio?

CARTER   I was wondering if you could help me with something.

CLAIRE   Um, okay.

CARTER   I have to write this paper for my Ethics class and I thought you would be good at the proof-reading thing. You know, read it over and tell me if all my periods are in the right place.

CLAIRE   Places.

CARTER   Yeah, stuff like that.

CLAIRE   How bad could it be? The boy was pre-law, right? Yeah, whatever. Carter has the grammar and usage of a tenth grader. His spelling is— Ellgh, sorry, there's bile in my mouth just now. I tore his paper to shreds, made it bleed with red ink, with circles and lines and arrows, thinking it would be the only time, that he'd freak at the possibility of asking me for help because I was just going to be mean about it. But the toolbox kept coming back.

CARTER   You're a lifesaver, Claire. A genius. I got an eighty-eight on my Ethics paper, and I know it's thanks to you.

CLAIRE   He brought me ice cream as a thank you. And then he brought his law school application. After which he fixed the CD player in my car, which was nice of him. Especially considering I wasn't being particularly nice to him. Suddenly it was like the three of us were dating. I didn't relish the idea of being the third wheel, but Bren and I somehow settled back into our old patterns. The difference being that Carter was there. Here. All the time. Tuesday at the dollar movie . . .

CARTER   It's the only way I'll see anything with Keanu Reeves. They should pay me fifty cents to sit through this crap.

CLAIRE   Wednesdays, grocery shopping and bad TV. Turns out Carter is a closet gourmet.

CARTER   Tonight you ladies will enjoy *American Idol* alongside my chicken pesto and linguine. I made the pesto myself.

CLAIRE   Someone give this boy a gold star for effort. Friday nights were the best nights because Carter, tolerable as he had become, had to work, teaching French to new missionaries. So Fridays were still mine, and Bren and I could be—us. Us, the way we were pre-Carter. There was one Friday when I almost told her. I remember it like—

We're watching *A Room with a View*. The Merchant Ivory one, of course. I've just eaten way too much pizza— I think Bren's had two slices to my six—and I'm just sitting. I'm not really paying attention to much of anything; I know the movie too well. For the first time in weeks, I take for granted the fact that she is here, with me, and that Carter is somewhere else. I'm content just to be sitting on the same ratty couch she is and talk about nothing, like we have hundreds of times before.

BRENNAN   I can't believe how young Helena Bonham Carter is in this. She has to be what, eighteen?

CLAIRE   Seventeen, I think. She was sixteen in *Lady Jane*.

BRENNAN   Who else was in that one?

CLAIRE   Westley from *The Princess Bride*.

BRENNAN   Right. And Captain Picard.

CLAIRE   Then she does something. Something absolutely—

BRENNAN *lies on the couch, her head in* CLAIRE'S *lap.*

It is lovely, and familiar. And somehow Gutsy Me comes out of hiding.

I've been thinking.

BRENNAN   If it's about why e. e. cummings is too good for capital letters, let's skip to the part where I don't care.

CLAIRE   It's about Carter.

BRENNAN   Hmm.

CLAIRE   I don't know if I like him.

BRENNAN   I know you don't.

CLAIRE   I mean, watching Daniel Day-Lewis bumbling through this movie, he's such a conceited twit, of course you want Helena to end up with Julian. You just do. And I kind of think that Carter is— Well—

BRENNAN   A conceited twit.

CLAIRE   Yes.

BRENNAN   So are you, in your own way. Sure, Carter can be full of himself. But he's also incredibly good to me. He's sweet, and he listens, and he wants me to be happy. Are you jealous?

CLAIRE   . . . Rather.

BRENNAN   I'll take that as a compliment.

CLAIRE   Then the second amazing thing happens.

BRENNAN *takes one of* CLAIRE'S *hands in her own.*

We sit so in near silence—the movie has faded to the dull buzz that can only come from an English comedy of manners too often watched—and I just stare at her hand in mine. A thousand thoughts pass behind my eyes and my throat is dry. Min-

Christie Clark as Brennan, Laurel Sandberg-Armstrong as Claire. New Play Project.
© 2009 Jen Jenkins.

utes go by, and she doesn't let go. I have to pee,
but I don't move, not an inch, not a muscle.

Bren, I . . . I don't hate Carter. I don't even really
dislike him, not anymore. He's kind of grown
on me, like mold, I don't know. I mean, at least
there are different kinds of mold. It's even pretty
sometimes. Fuzzy, you know? Look, what I hate
is seeing him with you because I— Let me get this
out, I have to get this out. Brennan, I love you.
I'm—in love with you.

. . . . . . Bren?

She looks so—and her weight on me is pleas-
antly warm and right. I can't wake her, not even
to repeat what I said. Not that I could repeat it.

Either way, it's a glorious two and a half minutes. At least, till her phone rings.

BRENNAN ... Hello? ... Hey, hi ... I'm fine, how are you? Sorry, I just— I must have fallen asleep.

CLAIRE Carter is off work. Bren goes into the kitchen to talk to him, likely planning to meet up at Denny's or IHOP or— Whatever.

When December rolled around I was sick to death of Provo. Of the valley, of the pollution, of stupid California drivers, and the fact that you can't buy a Coke on campus that has caffeine in it. Don't people realize that there is actually a difference in taste between the red can and the gold can? I was looking forward to going home like you wouldn't believe, just for the change of scenery. But aside from my four-month-old niece, nothing at home felt different, other than the fact that I couldn't see Brennan on a daily basis. I was walking under water; I could see everyone, and they could see me. But reaching out to them was so hard, like there was something between us at every step, at every juncture. Somehow I smiled and laughed with everyone else, but all the while I was thinking about Bren. She and Carter were planning to visit both sets of parents over the break, and that usually means a certain something is going to happen. Just a matter of time, right?

My sister was never someone I confided in, not really. I mean, she's three years younger, and growing up our conversations involved ear-shattering decibels and usually some kicking. But I figured if I told Natalie, the freak-out level would be so much lower than with Mom or Dad. I mean, since the one person in the world I would normally tell was the object of my—um, obsession? Affection? Never mind.

One morning, around six-thirty, I go downstairs to the kitchen.

NATALIE   You're up early.

CLAIRE   Force of habit. What about you?

NATALIE   Can't say no to Grace.

CLAIRE   She's lovely.

NATALIE   Isn't she? Here, take her.

CLAIRE   Can I?

NATALIE   Of course. Look out, she likes hair, playing with it and chewing on it and pulling it out.

CLAIRE   . . . Hey, Nat, can I ask you something? It's going to sound cheesy and stupid—

NATALIE   What is it?

CLAIRE   How did you know, about Tom? That he was the one?

NATALIE   You're right, that is cheesy.

CLAIRE   Was it something about him, or what?

NATALIE   He snores. I never thought I could marry a man who snores. Thing is, he sleeps so well. He's got one hand kind of flopped over, and his mouth is open just a little. Looks kinda like a puppy.

CLAIRE   What about before? Before you were married or engaged, even. I mean, how did you know you wanted to date him?

NATALIE   Why? Is there someone? Someone you're thinking about?

CLAIRE   . . . You could say that.

NATALIE   That was a heavy sigh. Is he hot?

CLAIRE   Um. I don't know.

NATALIE   You don't know if he's hot?

CLAIRE   Deep breath. This is a time for Gutsy Me. Be gutsy, screw the thoughtful.

I think I'm in love with someone that I shouldn't be.

NATALIE   Really. Who? Cardinal rule: never date your roommate's ex. Someone else's boyfriend?

CLAIRE   She's enjoying this. She's actually—she tries to joke about it.

NATALIE   It's not someone's husband, is it?

CLAIRE   Natalie, no.

NATALIE   Then who? You're either attracted to someone or you're not. It's really not that complicated.

CLAIRE   I think— I don't know.

NATALIE   How can you not know? Look, are you going to tell me or—

CLAIRE   It's—it's a her. It's Brennan.

Heidi Smith Anderson as Natalie, Jessica Myer as Claire. Echo Theatre. © 2013 Jaron Hermansen.

CLAIRE   She just looks at me, and I look down to find Grace staring up at me. Those little eyes . . .

NATALIE   You don't know that. I mean, you're not—

CLAIRE   I think I am—

NATALIE   Oh.

CLAIRE   Tell me what to do. I don't know what to do.

NATALIE   Don't you mean, what you shouldn't do?

CLAIRE   Um, the baby is—

NATALIE   Is she—?

CLAIRE   I don't know, she just started—

NATALIE   Here, give her to me.

CLAIRE   Nat, I—

NATALIE   Have you said anything to Mom or Dad?

CLAIRE   No.

NATALIE   Good. Don't. I mean— I have to—

CLAIRE   And she's gone. We manage to avoid each other for almost two days. Not that I'm trying too hard to be found, or that we were ever super close in the first place. When she's ready, Natalie finds me at the piano.

CLAIRE *picks out a few notes from "Angels We Have Heard on High."*

NATALIE *enters on the edge of the light. Eventually she joins* CLAIRE *at the piano. They try to play together, but the song quickly disintegrates into barely recognizable chords and the sisters share a laugh. After a bit:*

NATALIE   When was the last time you went out? With a guy?

CLAIRE   Freshman year. I went dutch to dinner and a movie with McKay Swim. We worked the same shift at the Bookstore.

NATALIE   So you were dating.

CLAIRE   McKay? Um, no. He told me I wasn't the kind of girl he would—marry.

NATALIE   He said that? After one date?

CLAIRE   BYU can be a weird place.

NATALIE   Yeah, it can. And that was your freshman year.

CLAIRE   Five years ago.

NATALIE   That was your last date?

CLAIRE   Yes. So I'm a social reject. What's your point?

NATALIE   Why haven't you asked guys out? You need to be assertive. Put yourself out there and someone will—

CLAIRE   This is me, Nat. When have I ever put myself out anywhere? I would much rather stay in, thank you very much.

NATALIE   Look where it got you.

CLAIRE   I didn't ask for this. I didn't wake up one morning and pray, "Father in Heaven, please make me gay."

NATALIE   Is that supposed to be funny?

CLAIRE   Would you rather it were true?

NATALIE   Maybe you just haven't met the right guy. I mean, you and Brennan have always been close. You've spent so much time together that it's not really a surprise that you've formed, um—an attachment.

CLAIRE   You sound like a page out of Jane Austen, minus the gentility.

NATALIE   What does that even mean?

CLAIRE   It doesn't matter. The point is, I haven't even thought about guys in a long time. I haven't thought of them as hot or cool or even— I just haven't.

NATALIE   There has to be something you're doing wrong.

CLAIRE   What? Tell me, what? I'm not a bad person, am I? I study and I pray, I try to go to the temple every week. I do my visiting teaching, I fast, I pay my tithing. I served an honorable mission. I believe in everything I've always believed in. I just—feel differently.

NATALIE   So, Brennan . . . Have you thought about— kissing her?

CLAIRE   Yes.

NATALIE   A lot?

CLAIRE   Thinking or kissing?

NATALIE   Never mind.

CLAIRE   This doesn't make me— This isn't a sin, all right? To love someone . . .

NATALIE   You'll find the right guy.

CLAIRE   Who is going to marry me?

NATALIE   Someone. You're so smart, and talented. You're beautiful—

CLAIRE   It's not the same. You're my sister. It's different when you or Mom or Dad says it. Or Bishop Gates, even. It's never a guy, on a date or whatever, telling me because he likes me or, Heaven forbid, loves me.

NATALIE   Never?

CLAIRE   Never. I've never had a serious relationship with a guy, Nat. I've gone out with a few, but only once or twice.

NATALIE   . . . So because guys don't ask you out, you think you're a lesbian.

CLAIRE   I hadn't thought of it in exactly those terms, and suddenly it all seemed foolish, and fake, that I was putting it on myself, like I was changing coats despite the summer heat. Did I make it all up? Have I simply spent so much time with Bren that I can't imagine spending time with anyone else? Maybe I just—like her so much that I always want to be in the same room with her. Was I just jealous that she and Carter had each other while I was destined for an eternity of third-wheel-ness?

Brennan called. On Christmas Eve, from her Mom's house in Mesa. Hearing her voice was really— Wow.

BRENNAN   Hi. How's Oregon?

CLAIRE   Fine. Arizona?

BRENNAN   Gorgeous. Seventy degrees and holding.

CLAIRE   Oh, don't tell me that.

BRENNAN   Can I tell you something else instead?

CLAIRE   Deep breath, here it comes.

BRENNAN   Carter's asked me to marry him.

CLAIRE   If you couldn't tell, Christmas was kind of a disaster.

BRENNAN   It's cliché, I know, but I so want to get married in June.

CLAIRE   Was she in love with him? It took me a year and a half to figure out what to major in. How could she possibly know after just four months that this was the man with whom she was meant to spend eternity?

BRENNAN   Claire, you're my best friend. Be my maid of honor. Please? . . . Claire?

CLAIRE   . . . Sorry, I think my cell is— It's snowing and— I'd love to. Of course I will.

I'm a terrible person, I'm a liar, I lied, the last thing in the world I wanted was to be a bridesmaid. But I knew she wanted me to say yes, so I said yes.

Can I just say, watching someone else date is boring. Reality TV works because some poor editor has to wade through hours of footage to piece together forty-five minutes of high drama. "Piece" being the key word. 95% of *Survivor* is just people sitting on an island. Boring. At least watching reality TV you can change the channel when things get slow or, well—awkward. When the drama is unfolding in your living room, you don't exactly enjoy that luxury.

BRENNAN   You're so not going to throw that out.

CARTER   What?

BRENNAN   It's glass.

CARTER   It's a jar. Peanut butter is gone, so I throw the jar away.

BRENNAN   No you don't. You recycle it.

CARTER   What for?

BRENNAN   You can't just throw it out.

CARTER   . . . So what? You want to keep pencils in it?

BRENNAN   No. I don't want it.

CARTER   Then what're you talking about?

BRENNAN   Killing the planet.

CARTER   It's. A. Jar.

CLAIRE   Yeah, that was a good one. Or how about . . .

CARTER   Doesn't taste like a burger.

BRENNAN   It's tofu.

CARTER   Ellgh.

CLAIRE   Those were the tiny things, the tiny things that couples call "little bumps in the road." But there were the not-so-tiny things, the questions that come up when two people attempt to combine their separate lives into one. Especially when you haven't been together that long in the first place.

CARTER   What's all this?

BRENNAN   Grad school applications. I've always dreamed of going to Columbia.

CARTER   Columbia, wow. That's great.

BRENNAN   Isn't it?

CARTER   Columbia's in New York.

BRENNAN   So?

CARTER   I'm applying to law schools on the West Coast.

BRENNAN   There are fantastic journalism programs in the West, sure. UC Berkeley, maybe. And maybe you could apply to a couple places back East too, just in case. You know, a fall-back plan?

CARTER   ... Sure. I mean, okay.

CLAIRE   Golly, this is awkward, I'm just going to sit on the couch and read my book and look like I'm not listening, how can I not be listening, but I can't look like I'm listening. The thing is, and I know it's crazy talk, but it was worse when they got along. I just— I couldn't handle it. If I walked into a room and they were cuddling on the couch, or paging through bridal magazines, or dozing through the closing credits of *The Count of Monte Cristo*, I would turn on my heel and go back the way I came. Because it—them—it didn't feel right. I split most of my free time that semester between my very small room and the stale air of the Humanities level of the library.

I quietly quit being the third wheel of the Brennan/Carter-mobile in February. I said I was busy, that I had papers to write, books to read. I read a lot, it's what I do. They didn't question—they didn't really even notice, they were so into each other, so that was okay. I tried not to think about it. For the first time in my life I avoided something I loved. I walked to school every morning to feel the pricking of the wind and enjoy the numbness in my face. It was hard to think about other things when my ears ached with the cold, and I knew walking up Seventh East toward campus why God had created winter, for this express reason. To let the outside deflect a little of what was going on inside. It was like I was back on my mission, and the only serious conversations I was having were with God. Which is okay, really, he's a very good listener, and he appreciates my word choice. I like to think he does, anyway.

Heavenly Father, make me stronger. Help me endure. Show me that Thou lovest me, that I'm worth something to Thee . . .

And He would. He still does. Tiny little miracles, just for me. My checking account staying out of the red, a surprise extension on an unfinished paper, a sale on clementines at Albertsons, the chance sighting of a cardinal outside my window. And always, that constant warmth in the center of my chest that told me I wasn't alone, not really. Though in my selfish, imperfect way, I couldn't help thinking it wasn't enough.

One day my phone rang. My phone actually rang. But it wasn't Brennan, it was Natalie. Something had happened and . . .

BRENNAN   Hi. You're not answering your cell.

CLAIRE   Sorry. I've been on the other line.

BRENNAN   What's going on?

CLAIRE Can you take me to the airport? I don't think
I should drive.

BRENNAN Sure. Of course.

CLAIRE She comes a little closer and I don't turn my
head, I don't let myself look at her, because I can
smell her. I can smell the Clinique Happy, and it's
not right, it's not right that I should want anything
for myself in this moment. In this moment when
my sister is . . .

BRENNAN What happened?

CLAIRE Grace was dead in her crib this morning.

BRENNAN I'm so sorry.

CLAIRE Tom's gone for work, and he's stuck, something about a really big storm. I'm going to stay
with Natalie; she shouldn't be alone—

She's at my elbow, and I have to tell myself:
Breathe. Breathe, like little Gracie can't.

She was just—she's gone. I don't understand.

BRENNAN I don't think we're supposed to.

Throughout the following, CLAIRE *and* BRENNAN *are
brought close together—incredibly close, within
inches—but never actually touch.*

CLAIRE Probably not. There are a lot of things I don't
understand.

I am unprepared. All too soon her arms are
around me, and Happy is in my nostrils and coat-

Christie Clark as Brennan, Laurel Sandberg-Armstrong as Claire. New Play Project. © 2009 Jen Jenkins.

ing the back of my throat, like she put too much on. But it's just that I haven't been this close to her in weeks and it's overwhelming, the sense of homecoming. I'm afraid something in me might just break, but I can't pull away. I turn my head just slightly, and her face is there, inches from mine. Then centimeters. Millimeters. Our cheeks touch for several seconds— Stolen time, starry nights, lilacs in May, little happy secrets . . .

I don't realize I'm kissing her until she pulls away.

BRENNAN   What are you—

CLAIRE   I'm sorry. I— I'm sorry.

BRENNAN   . . . . . . What time is your flight?

CLAIRE   Seven.

BRENNAN   Then we'd better go. I'll get my keys.

CLAIRE   It's rush hour, and we get stuck on I-15 around Murray for what feels like ages. Her hands can't stop moving, fidgeting, adjusting the radio, the air, the mirrors. Finally they stop, her knuckles white on the wheel. I just sit and want to die.

At the curb of Terminal One I say, Thanks. And she—

BRENNAN   ... ...

CLAIRE   She doesn't even look at me. She just— So I get out of the car, I walk away, and I get on a plane.

Nat? Natalie? The front door was open. Did you mean to leave it open? . . . I locked it, anyway.

NATALIE   Don't put your bag there. Put it in the spare room.

CLAIRE   Okay.

NATALIE   ... Claire ...

CLAIRE   Yeah.

NATALIE   Why— What are you doing here?

CLAIRE   You called, so I—

NATALIE   That's not what I mean. I mean, thanks, but . . .

CLAIRE   What?

NATALIE   We haven't—since Christmas. We haven't talked, and I know it's my fault. I just— You didn't have to come.

CLAIRE   Are you okay? I know that's a stupid question, but—

NATALIE   You came anyway.

CLAIRE   Of course I came.

More silence, but this time a different kind. I lie with my sister in the dark, I hold her while she cries. While we cry together.

I don't understand, Father. I don't— A baby, Grace is only a baby. Not old enough to sin, to even talk. It doesn't make sense, I can't get my head around it. Natalie is a good mother, she should be a mother. And I'm trying so hard, Heavenly Father. I'm trying to be good. I think I am good. Why this? Why this child? It's so unfair, so— Is it me? Is it some strange eye for an eye thing? I thought we were past the law of Moses, I didn't think my family would be punished for my— Is it even a sin? To wonder, to care? To want? That's where the sin comes in, doesn't it. The wanting. The fact that I want someone I'm not meant to have . . . Well, I'm not the one that put her there for the wanting, you know what I'm saying? . . . Forgive me, Father, for my selfishness. I don't know how I turned this to be about me, I didn't mean for that to happen.

I stayed with Natalie till the day after the funeral. I thought about calling Bren a whole mess of times, I even did the whole dial-all-but-the-last-number bit. Like you even need to do that with a smart phone, right? Ridiculous.

When I get home, Bren is at the kitchen table, studying. Looking at her, tasting Happy in the back of my throat—

BRENNAN Hi.

CLAIRE Hi.

BRENNAN I'm sorry about your niece, about Grace.

CLAIRE Thank you.

BRENNAN We should probably— We should talk.

CLAIRE Okay.

You know, for needing to talk, there's a lot of talk that's not happening right now and I just wonder if—

BRENNAN Claire, I . . .

CLAIRE Yeah?

BRENNAN I love Carter.

CLAIRE . . . Okay.

BRENNAN He's asked me to marry him and I've accepted. That's not going to change. But I need to know something. I just need to— Never mind, I don't want to know.

We—you and I— I don't even know what to call it. It's just—we can't—it can't happen. You need to find someone who will make you happy.

CLAIRE You think I don't know that? It hurts me like you cannot believe, to feel this way, to be this lonely. At the same time, I don't know if I want to kneel at the altar with anyone. Something is missing. On the one hand, it's the guy. On the other, it's me.

BRENNAN   Nothing is wrong with you.

CLAIRE   Isn't there?

BRENNAN   Of course not.

CLAIRE   I don't think about sex. I don't fantasize, I don't wonder, I don't masturbate. I don't think about men as physical counterparts, I just think about them as—men. Guys. People in front of you in the check-out line who beat you to the last cookie and steal your parking spot and don't shower nearly enough. That's all. A husband is supposed to be your best friend, someone to hold your hand in good or ill. Bren, you're my best friend. You always have been. You're the only person I want to spend time with.

BRENNAN   ... ... So you've thought about sex. With me.

CLAIRE   No.

BRENNAN   I don't understand.

CLAIRE   I've thought about kissing you. About holding you while you sleep. I've thought abo—

BRENNAN   Stop. I can't hear th— You're my best friend, and I love you for that. As a friend. But I don't know if we can do that anymore.

CLAIRE   You joking? You don't think I can be enough of an adult to maintain our friendship?

BRENNAN   I'm moving out. I'll find someone to take my spot in the house.

CLAIRE   The semester is half over, no one is looking for—

BRENNAN   Then I'll stay at my cousin's and pay the rent. I just— I don't think we should live together.

CLAIRE   You think I'm going to come into your room in the middle of the night?

BRENNAN   What you're suggesting, what you're asking of me—

CLAIRE   Am I ever going to see you again after you're married?

BRENNAN   And suddenly this has everything to do with what you want.

CLAIRE   . . . I— I have to—

BRENNAN   Are you okay?

CLAIRE   Little dizzy, no big deal.

BRENNAN   You're all— You're kind of ashen. Are you—

CLAIRE   I'm freaking out, and I've been fasting. Bad combination.

BRENNAN   Fasting? What for?

CLAIRE   What do you think?

BRENNAN   Sorry. Of course. I just— How long? Your fast, how long has it been going on?

CLAIRE   On and off this week.

BRENNAN   You've been fasting all week?

CLAIRE   On and off, I said. I've been eating dinner. Sometimes.

BRENNAN   Claire, that's not healthy.

CLAIRE   I'm feeling a little short in the clarity department. I'm trying to figure things out. Fasting is supposed to clear the mind and— I didn't know what else to do. I meant to tell you so much sooner. But then Natalie's baby, and Carter—

BRENNAN   Yes, Carter. You don't like him.

CLAIRE   He's a little self-involved.

BRENNAN   He's used to being right.

CLAIRE   He drives a Lincoln Navigator.

BRENNAN   It was a present from his parents, when he got into law school.

CLAIRE   What will you and he discuss over dinner? Are you laying ground rules, are you going to limit your conversation to "Please pass the liberty cabbage"? How does he feel about the GOP? Does he go deer hunting? Collect guns?

BRENNAN   I had no idea you were this bitter.

CLAIRE   You don't love him.

BRENNAN   You're just saying that because—

CLAIRE   It's nothing to do with me.

BRENNAN   You're kidding, right?

CLAIRE This all happened so fast, you and Carter— You think you're in love with him.

BRENNAN This isn't— I have to go. I'll email you about the sublease.

CLAIRE I should be the one to go. Nothing's going to be the same, and it's my fault.

BRENNAN Where will you go?

CLAIRE Seattle. Natalie.

BRENNAN You're going to leave? School?

CLAIRE For a while.

BRENNAN You can't just—

CLAIRE Hon, I love you. I would do just about anything for you. But I can't stay and watch you marry him. I should, but I'm not strong enough.

I didn't stop, I didn't let myself. I withdrew from the university. I filled my car with clothes, with books, with movies. Didn't really look, just moved to keep moving. And I drove to Seattle.

NATALIE I thought that was your car. What are you—? I expected a visit, but not so soon.

CLAIRE Surprise. I was thinking about looking for a job. Any ideas?

Nat had worked at a Borders before having Grace, and she introduced me to her old manager. I had a little miracle; he hired me on the spot. It didn't take long to settle into a routine. Natalie didn't ask questions, she just opened doors. Things were okay, they were fine. Because I kept moving. Except for the hole in me, the void that I kept trying to fill with work and writing and books—thirty percent is a dangerous discount—but nothing stayed, nothing took root. The hole didn't shrink, but it didn't exactly grow, either. It just—was. A hole in my being, a hole where Brennan should have been. Except that I tried to cut her out, neatly, with those sharp little shears Nat uses to cut out photos for her scrapbooks. Though the photo is gone, I can still see Brennan. Right there. Like— Those months in Seattle, they kind of blur together when I think back on them. They were empty. I went to work, I came home, and I read, like always.

NATALIE   What're you reading?

CLAIRE   *Persuasion.*

NATALIE   Again?

CLAIRE   Uh huh.

NATALIE   I don't understand how you can do that, read things over and over. I read something, maybe I like it, and that's all. I don't even like to own books.

CLAIRE   Oh, I know.

NATALIE   It must be good, if you're reading it for the zillionth time.

CLAIRE   It's one of the best. You can borrow it, if you want. You'd like it. It's a love story, classic.

NATALIE   Happy ending?

CLAIRE   Do you want to know?

NATALIE   I need one, I think, even if it's fictional.

CLAIRE   Here. It's a good ending, I promise.

NATALIE   Don't you want to finish it first?

CLAIRE   I practically have it memorized. Take your time.

NATALIE   . . . I won't need a dictionary, will I?

CLAIRE   You shouldn't.

NATALIE   Thanks.

CLAIRE   No problem.

> My sister and I have always been good at giving each other—space. She did her thing, and I did mine. But now we had both endured a heartbreak, and that changed the air between us. Leveled the playing field? I don't know. We had something in common, something we hadn't before. We each understood the other's sorrow and then, suddenly, the incongruities in taste, in personality. . . . It all seemed superficial. After all, we both want what everyone wants: that elusive happy ending. What I've realized, though, is that a "happy ending"—that's a bit of a tall order for every day. I mean, ultimately, sure, you want to end happily. But at the same time, who wants to end? Either you're happy and ended, or you're not quite happy, but at least still living. It's a literal take, I know, but that's where I have to find consolation, in the fact that I'm still living. Day to day, hour to hour, breath to breath, just—living.

One day I come home for lunch. Nat, I'm home.

NATALIE   There's mail for you. Mom sent it up.

CLAIRE   Not like there's ever anything good. Credit card, credit card, phone bill, student loan, junk junk junk— Oh. Um . . .

NATALIE   How's work? Claire? What's the matter?

CLAIRE   It's a vellum envelope, addressed in calligraphy.

A light on BRENNAN.

BRENNAN   To Ms. Claire Allen and Guest. Brennan Ashley Chandler and Carter Dallas Weston have chosen to be sealed for time and all eternity in the Mesa LDS Temple on Friday, the twenty-third of June. You are cordially invited to attend a reception held in their honor.

CLAIRE   The invitation is an ivory card with a linen finish; timeless, classic. When I pull it out, a photograph and a slip of paper fall to the floor, fluttering like a lost soul. In the photo, Brennan and Carter grin cheek to cheek, posed against Y Mountain in matte finished black and white. On the slip of paper, written in a familiar hand, are three little words.

BRENNAN   Stop me. Please.

CLAIRE   Keys, where are my keys? I just had them—

NATALIE   Hold on a second. What's going on?

CLAIRE   Friday, the wedding is Friday morning.

NATALIE   Tomorrow. Claire, wait—

CLAIRE   I have to go. I'll call you from the road.

NATALIE   Do you even know where you're going?

NATALIE AND BRENNAN   Claire.

CLAIRE   When Nat called me, I heard Brennan's voice. Was I going crazy? Was I finally losing it? I just got in the car. I grabbed my wallet and a six-pack of Coke and I drove to Mesa. I don't know what I expected to do. If this was a scene out of a romantic comedy I might just burst into the wedding and yell "Wait!" Do people actually ever do that? Real people, I mean? I drove all night. Sometime around four in the morning the car was wavering, weaving a little in the lane; I hunched over the wheel, straining my eyes to keep them open. It's a miracle that I didn't get pulled over since I was pushing eighty-five and ninety most of the time. Good little Honda kept on trucking. I only stopped to fill the tank, to pick up sugar and caffeine. Getting to Mesa wasn't a problem. But I had never been to the Mesa Temple, so once I hit the sprawl of the suburbs—and Mesa is basically one gigantic suburb— I had no idea where to go. I guess I thought I would just find it. I mean, it's a temple, how can you miss it, right? But I wandered up and down streets for more than an hour, frustrated to tears before I let myself ask for directions. When I find the temple, there is a crowd out front. From a distance, I recognize Brennan's parents. There are people everywhere, aunts and uncles and cousins, and a photographer, but where—

Applause. Cheers as Mr. and Mrs. Carter Weston step out into the Arizona sunshine.

It is incredibly hot. I sit sweating in my car in the parking lot, for I don't know how long. I don't roll down the windows, I just sit in the heat, my hair going stringy and my clothes damp. Breathing out of my mouth, sucking in more heat than air. Watching from across the lot as the wedding party poses on the grounds, as they split into groups and drive away. For the luncheon and, eventually, the reception. I guess. I could go, to say "hi" or whatever, but I know somehow that if I see her it will be worse. For her, for me. It'll just spoil the day, and so many people will—talk. Secrets, right? Bren deserves better than that. I deserve better than that. So I turn the key, get back on the 202, head north.

On the drive home a grey film hangs over everything despite the sun. I have a roaring headache, I'm starving, and a shower can only be a good thing. I don't think about driving, I just do it, totally on autopilot, the speedometer holding steady at sixty-five. I sit back, both hands on the wheel, elbows relaxed, eyes half-closed. Eventually my right hand falls away from the wheel. My foot is on the gas. Seventy. Seventy-five. It's a straight stretch of highway. Heat shimmering, hovering just above the pavement, blurring the horizon. Not a lot of traffic. I'm alone in the middle of the desert; how appropriate. Eighty. The fingers of my left hand relax. Eighty-five. It'd be so easy to just—let go of everything. So I do. I drop my hand from the wheel altogether. Ninety. The car starts to veer into the left lane. Ninety-five. I look down the hood of the Honda through the haze of heat, at the shallow ditch running between the two sections of freeway, and I—

I couldn't go through with it. I took the wheel in both hands and turned it to the right. Took my foot off the gas. I did make it home. How? I'll say divine intervention, and you'll likely smile at that, but it's what I know.

The hole is still there, ragged along the edges, and I look for something—maybe someone—to fill it. Eventually. But I do have a slip of paper that I carry with me everywhere I go. A slip of paper blank except for three little words. It's funny, it's like it's enough that she asked. That she—considered me enough to ask.

Stolen time, starry nights, lilacs in May, little happy secrets. You know mine now. There are no more.

Black. End of play.

Pilot Program

a supposition
by Melissa Leilani Larson

Marriage is so unlike everything else.
　　　　　　　　　　　　　　—George Eliot, *Middlemarch*

What is your favorite word? "And. It is so hopeful."
　　　　　　　　　　　　　　—Margaret Atwood

Pilot Program received its world premiere at Plan-B Theatre Company (planbtheatre.org) in Salt Lake City, Utah from April 9–19, 2015, with the following cast:

Abigail	April Fossen
Jacob	Mark Fossen
Heather	Susanna Florence

Directed by Jerry Rapier. Sound by Cheryl Ann Cluff, costumes by Phillip R. Lowe, lighting by Jesse Portillo, set by Randy Rasmussen, props by Allison Smith. Stage managed by Jennifer Freed.

Settings

The play is a hypothetical set in the near future: the story begins in January 2020.

Most of the scenes, unless otherwise indicated, take place in the Husten home: a handsome, airy house in the Avenues in Salt Lake City, Utah.

There are a number of shorter scenes that don't require major scene shifts; these are meant to be suggestive rather than literal, driven by light and Abigail's narration.

Characters (2 W, 1 M)

ABIGAIL: Early 40s. A writer and professor. Warm, discerning, pensive.

JACOB: Early to mid-40s. Abigail's husband of 14 years. Reticent, constant, agreeable.

HEATHER: Early 30s. Abigail's friend and former student. Impetuous, bright, loyal.

Production notes

All of the characters are practicing Latter-day Saints (Mormons), which should be taken into account in regard to costume and behavior.

Sometimes silence is everything.

A set of ellipsis points (. . .) indicates a brief pause, perhaps a hesitation, especially at the beginning of a line. A double set (. . . . . .) indicates a significantly longer pause.

Lights rise on ABIGAIL. *She wears a dressy winter coat over her Sunday best. She is isolated in a simple, cool light—we'll call it her blogging light. She composes a blog entry, addressing the audience.*

ABIGAIL   The internet is a cemetery of unfinished blogs. It happens a lot: people start a blog to tell one important, personal story, but never get around to sharing any others—if they even finish one in the first place. Most are left hanging, one or two or three brief entries that really only begin to scratch the surface.

Sometimes story dictates medium, and this one— it wanted to find eternal life in the chalky green of motherboards and the vast yellow/gray space of the internet. I imagine cyberspace to be gray—not as cold or endless as black. Just space, in which stories and images can live infinitely. Where they can hide in little corners waiting for the proper search engine optimization, the right Google search or the right Bing— What is a Bing? Does anyone actually ever use it? What if it becomes the household verb that Google has? "Bing-ing" sounds like something teenagers do in the abandoned stacks of a high school library. No, my children won't grow up to Bing anything. My children—

I don't have any children. I probably won't. It's the way things are.

Lights shift to a living room. Comfortably tidy. Shabby chic. Books are everywhere.

A key turns in a lock and ABIGAIL *moves with the light to the living room.* JACOB HUSTEN *enters. He's in a suit and tie. Very nice.*

They stand so for a moment in the semi-dark. Silence. Finally he switches on a lamp. The silence continues. Neither moves for what seems like the longest time. What exactly has happened here?

JACOB   Abby—

ABIGAIL   Hungry?

JACOB   No.

ABIGAIL   I'm starving.

JACOB   What would you like?

ABIGAIL   You don't have to make anything.

JACOB   It's no trouble.

ABIGAIL   Leftovers are fine.

JACOB   The other night—

ABIGAIL   The other night at Tam's. Yes. Perfect. It's actually better after a day or two in the fridge. Sure you don't want some?

JACOB   You go ahead.

ABIGAIL disappears into the kitchen off. JACOB *stands for a moment. A bit shell-shocked.*

JACOB   *(calling)* Abby?

ABIGAIL   *(from off)* Yeah?

April Fossen as Abigail, Mark Fossen as Jacob. Plan-B Theatre. © 2015 Rick Pollock.

JACOB   **Never mind.**

ABIGAIL *comes back in. She still has her coat on.*

ABIGAIL   **What?**

JACOB   **Nothing. I said never mind.**

ABIGAIL   **All right.**

JACOB   **Do you want to—?**

ABIGAIL   **Not yet.**

JACOB   **You seem like you're handling it all right.**

ABIGAIL   **Don't worry. I'm not.**

JACOB   I didn't choose this.

ABIGAIL   No. But it most assuredly chose you.

JACOB   We don't have to say yes.

ABIGAIL   We told them we'd think about it.

JACOB   Which we are. But if we decide not to—

ABIGAIL   What happens?

JACOB   Nothing. We go back to being us.

ABIGAIL   Just us.

JACOB   Just us.

ABIGAIL   We don't get . . .

JACOB   What?

ABIGAIL   Disfellowshipped. Or something. Unfriended?

JACOB   For exercising our agency? Of course not.

ABIGAIL   This is the kind of thing you read about. Hear about happening to other people.

JACOB   They were disappointed, I think. That we didn't answer then and there.

ABIGAIL   Would they have been less disappointed if we had said "No" then and there?

JACOB   We wouldn't be the first.

ABIGAIL   That makes me feel better.

JACOB   If you want to say no, we'll say no.

ABIGAIL   You say that, but. . . . Another wife. Can you even . . .?

JACOB .. .. Come sit down. At least take off your coat.

ABIGAIL Stop trying to make me comfortable.

JACOB I was just trying to—

ABIGAIL You were just trying to be nice. You're a nice guy, the good guy. Did you ever think that maybe that's the reason this happened to us in the first place?

JACOB Sorry?

ABIGAIL You're such a good guy, Jake. You exceed expectation. On your mission, with the Young Men, in the bishopric. Now the High Council—

JACOB I just do what they ask me to.

ABIGAIL So like you.

JACOB Like you've turned down a calling. *(Off her look:)* What?

ABIGAIL Two years ago, when Wendy Rove had her back surgery. They asked me to sub for her and teach the Beehive class. But I knew those girls would drive me crazy. Can you imagine? I had guilt about it; Wendy was always super nice to me. But I knew that if I taught that class for a month, it would drag into two, and then six, and the next thing you know it's been three years surrounded by bleating 13-year-old girls who just don't know when to shut up.

JACOB You never said anything about it.

ABIGAIL Because I knew you'd look at me like that.

JACOB　There's no look. I'm not judging you.

ABIGAIL　Not intentionally.

JACOB　You know me better than that.

ABIGAIL　. . . Sorry. I didn't tell you because there was nothing to tell. I didn't want to do it so I said no.

JACOB　Sometimes the calling is more for you than for anyone else.

ABIGAIL　And this calling? Is it for you then? Or for me? Is it going to make me a better person? Stronger or—whatever?

JACOB　Maybe.

ABIGAIL　I know what my strengths are. Talking to tweens about chastity is not one of them.

JACOB　You're a cool working woman. Girls need role models like you.

ABIGAIL　Cool?

JACOB　The coolest.

ABIGAIL　You're kissing up. And it's working. Here's the thing. They don't want me in this scenario. I'm the broken one. They want you.

JACOB　Don't.

ABIGAIL　I'm not being self-deprecating. I'm being truthful. They want you because you're good. The good sort. You're one of the youngest guys on the High Council.

JACOB　So?

ABIGAIL　Everyone looks forward to the day you come and speak. Your jokes are actually funny. Unlike the boring old guys.

JACOB　Ssh.

ABIGAIL　Who's going to hear us? No one. This is a safe space. I hope so, anyway. We can be honest here. Truthful.

JACOB　Truthful. Like saying you're broken.

ABIGAIL　*(shrugging)* Well. There's some comfort in knowing I'm not the only one. Connie Reid is leaving her husband because they have too many children.

JACOB　I'm not supposed to discuss these things.

ABIGAIL　You always feel better after you tell me. You know it.

JACOB　Not really.

ABIGAIL　Usually you want to.

JACOB　This is too tight.

ABIGAIL　Here, let me.

She loosens his tie and undoes the top button of his shirt. It's a loving gesture. Perhaps a little sensual.

JACOB　Thanks.

ABIGAIL　I suppose we'll be the source of gossip soon enough. What a story.

JACOB They're going public sooner than I thought they would.

ABIGAIL In which case, we can only talk about it if we say yes.

JACOB At least they want us to talk about it. Your blog—

ABIGAIL I'm not going to blog about this.

JACOB You're always looking for something to write about. Don't tell me the restoration of polygamy is too blasé for your readers.

ABIGAIL And if we say no?

JACOB Then we say no.

ABIGAIL Will people know?

JACOB Why should they? Not even I knew about the Beehives.

ABIGAIL The Young Women's President knew. The looks she shot me during sacrament that week— they could cut glass. Who knows who she told. Before the assignment came she told me, "I've had my eye on you." What does that even mean? It creeped me out. I said no way in Hades. And my pretentious, professorial self meant it.

JACOB You, pretentious?

ABIGAIL That's what you're taking away?

JACOB How many callings have you turned down?

ABIGAIL Just the two.

JACOB   Two?

ABIGAIL   When we first got married they wanted me in the nursery.

JACOB   I never knew about any of this.

ABIGAIL   It wasn't worth mentioning. Anyway, now you know.

JACOB   Do you think I care? Really?

ABIGAIL   Probably not. Sometimes it takes a long time to get to know someone.

JACOB   Worship is a personal thing.

ABIGAIL   I've always been good at assuming that someone, somewhere, is judging me.

JACOB   When have I ever judged you?

ABIGAIL   You haven't. You don't. It's just my first thought. I can't help thinking that someone is judging me. All of the time.

JACOB   That's why you can't even sit in the same room with someone while they read something you've written.

ABIGAIL   Ugh, no. Can't stand it.

JACOB   It's kind of adorable.

ABIGAIL   Don't start.

JACOB   I know what I signed on for.

ABIGAIL   Do you, though? We're being asked to completely turn our lives upside down.

JACOB   Could be worse.

ABIGAIL   Beth in *Little Women*.

JACOB   I was thinking more along the lines of Job.

ABIGAIL   Right. Pestilence and boils.

JACOB   You see? Worse.

ABIGAIL   What if it's a test? To see what we'll say?

JACOB   What for?

ABIGAIL   I don't know. To see what crazy things they can ask us to do before we stand up and say no. If Elder Holland stood up in General Conference and told you to go out and move Mount Timpanogos, would you? If it is a test— What happens next? Do we get a gold star for saying "yes," and then get sent on our merry way?

JACOB   Elder Holland wouldn't actually do that.

ABIGAIL   Five years ago I wouldn't have expected the area authority to call us to be part of a plural marriage.

JACOB   Point taken.

ABIGAIL   God wants you to be a father. Who am I to stand in the way of that?

JACOB   You're my wife.

ABIGAIL   Three miscarriages. No luck with in vitro, or adoption. Maybe I'm the wrong wife.

JACOB   You're being ridiculous. The things you're saying tonight are—

ABIGAIL   What? Should I count my blessings? Should I thrill at the fact that we've been asked to join, of all things, a pilot program?

JACOB   The Church has never been good at naming things. Look. I'll call President Fleet. I'll tell him no. We'll do it tonight.

ABIGAIL   Have I've done something wrong?

JACOB   God isn't refusing you children because you're a sinner.

ABIGAIL   Not a sinner. Just a selfish, cynical, liberal workaholic.

JACOB cracks a smile.

JACOB   Those are only sins right here. Nowhere else. You're the most beautiful, cynical, liberal, work-aholic I've ever known. You're good, Abby. You are good.

ABIGAIL   You're the one they want, remember.

JACOB   I wish you wouldn't— We're together. A pack-age deal.

ABIGAIL   I know.

JACOB   They said to think about it, so we'll think about it. You and I both.

ABIGAIL   So strange that a question with a single-sylla-ble answer could be so complicated.

JACOB   Like a proposal.

ABIGAIL   That was different. I didn't think twice about it.

JACOB   Really.

ABIGAIL   It was a gut reaction. You asked me to marry you. My instinct told me to say "Yes," so I did. No doubts, no hesitations. I didn't know that I should. I felt that I should. Didn't hurt that you were hot, and that we could have a decent conversation. If I had thought about it too long, I would have talked myself out of it.

JACOB   No you wouldn't.

ABIGAIL   I'm not saying it would have been better or any-thing. Of course it wouldn't. But sometimes you have to go with your gut.

JACOB   Maybe. Maybe not. You didn't say no to the stake president.

ABIGAIL   So?

JACOB   Why didn't you tell him no? Then and there? You told the bishop no on the spot. About the Beehives. But now. This—

She is distressed. Agitated.

You're thinking about it. You're actually thinking about—

ABIGAIL   It doesn't make sense, I know it doesn't. Forty-five minutes later, I'm tied in knots. I'm angry and confused and all over the place. But the moment that he asked, in that second, that breath hanging in the air between him and me— There was a blos-som of warmth. A burst of— I don't know. Faith? Maybe it was the Spirit, maybe it was my imagination. But I felt it. That it—this—was the right thing. It was completely terrifying. And now I want to deny that it happened, but I can't. I can't.

JACOB   So your gut is telling you—

ABIGAIL   You didn't feel it.

JACOB   *(simple and straight up)* No. I didn't.

ABIGAIL   . . . . . . What if we were to do it?

JACOB   You're not serious.

ABIGAIL   I'm pretty sure I'm not kidding.

Silence.

JACOB   Abby . . .

But he doesn't know where the sentence is going. He approaches her. Removes her coat. She lets him.

I didn't sign on to have children with anyone else. I married you.

ABIGAIL   Listen. If—if you're supposed to be the next Abraham—

JACOB   Abraham?

ABIGAIL   Progeny numbered like the sands of the sea. Stars in the sky. It has to start somewhere. There has to be a first.

JACOB   I'm not a prophet, I'm not a patriarch. I'm just a guy. I work in PR. I like peanut butter. I just want to be with you.

ABIGAIL   I have an idea. Someone we should call.

JACOB   Who?

ABIGAIL   Heather. Heather Mendoza.

JACOB   Heather Mendo— Is she one of your students?

ABIGAIL   My best student. Don't you remember? She came over all the time. She loaned you that book on Diego Rivera.

JACOB   I remember the book.

ABIGAIL   You should call her.

JACOB   Why?

ABIGAIL   Because she would be good for us. She would be—she's an ideal candidate. If you're going to take another wife, the least I get is to choose her.

JACOB   This is surreal.

ABIGAIL   Heather is smart. She's pretty. She's young. Younger. And she's single. We already get along. If we were to bring in a stranger . . . I don't know if I could do that. And dating. Do they expect you to actually date someone?

JACOB   I don't know. This isn't exactly the nineteenth century. Did Brigham Young bring prospective wives home to meet the Mrs.? Mrses? Ses?

ABIGAIL   I don't know if he did, but he should have. It makes sense that he would.

JACOB   Sense is the last thing any of this makes.

ABIGAIL   We need to make our own sense. We need to make this work for us. It could be a gift. A blessing. We could be a family.

JACOB   We are—

ABIGAIL   Not completely.

JACOB   This is what your gut is telling you.

ABIGAIL   It hasn't been wrong yet.

JACOB   Get married again. Without you leaving or dying or— I need a minute.

ABIGAIL   If we're going to do it, we should do it. Meet the challenge head on.

JACOB   Without thinking about it.

ABIGAIL   We've done too much of that already.

She takes out her phone. Scrolls through her contacts.

JACOB   We'll have to submit her name to the stake president. They'll probably want to vet her.

ABIGAIL   I'm sure they'll give her the third degree. But no one has to know if we just happen to invite her over first.

JACOB   How can you be so sure it'll work out?

ABIGAIL   Heather is great. She's like a sister to me. What?

JACOB   I'd like to at least have a conversation with her. You know, before I ask her to marry me.

ABIGAIL   Do you want to call her? Or should I?

The lights shift and JACOB *exits.* ABIGAIL *writes another blog post.*

I called Heather and left a voicemail. Just like that. I couldn't help myself. She was working in San Francisco, at a publishing house where I'd helped her get an internship during grad school. It was less than an hour before she called me back, and the next thing I knew she was on a plane. I didn't know what I expected her to say. I didn't even know what I was going to ask her. I just thought, if there needs to be someone else— Why not someone just like me?

The doorbell rings. ABIGAIL *goes to the door and* HEATHER *enters.*

HEATHER   Oh my gosh, it's freezing.

ABIGAIL   Yeah, it's terrible. Ice on everything. I'm amazed you made it up the walk. We keep waiting for the icicles to drop and kill someone.

HEATHER   They're huge.

ABIGAIL   Right? Anyway, come on in.

The two women regard each other.

HEATHER   Wow. Hi.

ABIGAIL   You're here. I can't believe it.

HEATHER   Why are we being awkward? So strange.
Come here.

They hug.

ABIGAIL   It's so good to see you.

HEATHER   It's good to be seen.

ABIGAIL   Come in. Have a seat. Jake will be home any
minute.

HEATHER   Thanks.

ABIGAIL   You've been busy.

HEATHER   So have you. I love your blog. It's my sanctuary.
I read it every day and think, "Wow, I know her."

ABIGAIL   Hush.

HEATHER   It's true. I've converted people to reading your
stuff. You've made me start my own.

ABIGAIL   AmidTheHeather.com. It's clever.

HEATHER   Not too precious?

ABIGAIL   It's perfect. What else could you possibly call it?

HEATHER   I'm just getting started, of course. Nowhere
near your level. Oh, Abby. Your book—

ABIGAIL   It's not that big a deal.

HEATHER   It's an amazingly big deal. A huge deal. It's
colossal.

ABIGAIL   It's just a book.

HEATHER   Right. It's just a book published by Vintage. Abby, the early reviews are killer.

ABIGAIL   I don't dare read them. I get too nervous.

HEATHER   Still?

ABIGAIL   I don't write for other people to read it; that's just a lucky by-product. I write because I have to. To clear my head, or work through a problem. It's just how my mind works. It'll probably always be strange to know someone other than me wants to read something of mine.

HEATHER   I hadn't realized how much I miss this place. You have the same lamps. This rug . . .

ABIGAIL   I'm sure everything is pretty much the same. More books, if such a thing is possible. How was your flight?

HEATHER   Fine. Quick, which was a blessing. Feels like it's been ages since I've been in Salt Lake.

ABIGAIL   Almost three years.

HEATHER   And yet everything feels the same.

ABIGAIL   That's the funny thing about this place. It always feels like home. I'm sorry, we should have come to get you.

HEATHER   Oh, no. I got a rental. I have to drive myself. I'm guessing the trains are still running blithely on their own timetable.

ABIGAIL   At least you can take the FrontRunner from Ogden to Cedar City. If you're so inclined.

HEATHER   Abby— Are you— Is everything okay?

ABIGAIL   Yes. Why shouldn't it be?

HEATHER   The other night on the phone. You sounded distant. Away. I mean, I was thrilled to hear from you. But it felt so out of the blue.

ABIGAIL   I know. I'm sorry. Things have been so busy lately. The book has been taking up a lot of time. I've been exiling poor Jake while I've been working. But I don't think he minds too much since he got his new Playstation.

HEATHER   Are you and Jake . . .?

ABIGAIL   Jake and I are fine. Promise. I just wanted to see you. Tell me about you. About work.

HEATHER   Oh, work is work. I don't think anyone really understands how satisfying it is to copy edit a manuscript. And when the book hits its second printing, you can point out the pages where you fought tooth and nail for those paragraph breaks and say, "I did this."

ABIGAIL   That's great. Really. I'm very proud.

HEATHER   I have you to thank for it. Your recommendation opened so many doors.

ABIGAIL   You deserve everything good that's come your way. Once they met you it was just a matter of time before they made an offer.

HEATHER   How's the department?

ABIGAIL   Oh, political and dramatic. As per always.

HEATHER   Always.

ABIGAIL   Teaching is— I mean, it's always rewarding. But there are days when you wonder if any of them are even listening.

HEATHER   When your book takes off, you can retire from teaching all famous and independently wealthy.

ABIGAIL   A likely story.

HEATHER   It's going to happen. And then you can hire me to be your assistant and help with your memoirs.

ABIGAIL   Ha!

HEATHER   You think I'm joking.

ABIGAIL   It's a very pretty possibility. Prettier for its unlikelihood.

HEATHER   Well, if you ever needed me, you know I'd drop everything to run over. You know I would.

ABIGAIL   I know.

HEATHER   I mean it. I should have called.

ABIGAIL   Sorry?

HEATHER   When I read your post about your miscarriage. I should have called.

ABIGAIL   Oh. Yes. Which one?

HEATHER   Which—?

ABIGAIL   I've had three.

HEATHER   Abby—

ABIGAIL   Don't. I didn't say it to— Don't feel bad. It's no one's fault. I want you to know. I don't want us to have any—secrets.

HEATHER   I had no idea.

ABIGAIL   I didn't post about all of them. It's a stupid reason, but— They all sounded the same. The same words all came out in the same order. How many different ways can you say "heartbreak"? English is funny that way. A dozen ways to say something is wonderful but the ways to say "sad" . . . They all sound the same. Heartbroken. Heartrending. Heartsick. Everything comes back to the heart. No one ever says, "I'm heart-happy." Anyway, I was sad. What else is there to say? I was frustrated that I couldn't write about it differently. I didn't want to repeat myself. Didn't want to think about it anymore.

HEATHER   I wish you had told me sooner.

ABIGAIL   I didn't want to distract you. You have your own life to lead. Your own projects, your own path. I just— Oh, this was a terrible idea.

HEATHER   What is?

JACOB enters, just home from work.

ABIGAIL   Jake.

JACOB   Hey.

He kisses her. It's nice. He tries for another, but . . .

ABIGAIL   Jake . . .

JACOB   What?

ABIGAIL   Heather's here.

JACOB   Oh. Right. Sorry. Heather. Hi.

> *We could possibly have one of the most awkward handshakes of all time happening right now. Just saying.*

HEATHER   Hi.

JACOB   Hi.

> *Silence.*

ABIGAIL   He remembers.

JACOB   I remember. I didn't think— Thanks for coming.

HEATHER   Of course. I'm glad for the excuse to visit. If there was ever a professor who changed my life, it was Abby.

JACOB   I'm not surprised.

ABIGAIL   Heather's very talented in her own right.

JACOB   She would have to be. To keep up with you.

ABIGAIL   Don't.

HEATHER   It's true.

JACOB   I knew it.

ABIGAIL   Stop it. Both of you.

JACOB　Sorry I'm late. Can I get you anything, Heather? Water? Pellegrino?

HEATHER　Sure, that'd be great. Whatever's easiest.

He exits into the kitchen. HEATHER *watches him go.*

You guys. You two. You don't look like you've changed a bit.

ABIGAIL　I don't know that we have.

HEATHER　That's fabulous.

ABIGAIL　You think so?

HEATHER　So many people get married for the wrong reasons. Too fast, outside pressure . . . You guys are the real deal.

ABIGAIL　Have you . . . Is there someone? In your life?

HEATHER　*(lightly)* That trail of shattered dreams goes off in a direction I no longer choose to travel.

ABIGAIL　Really.

HEATHER　I have things to do. Places to visit. I'm doing three months in the Alps come June. Just me, Margaret Atwood, and Switzerland.

ABIGAIL　Sounds lovely.

JACOB *re-enters with water glasses for all.*

HEATHER　*(to* JACOB*)* You know, I used to have the biggest crush on you.

JACOB *and* ABIGAIL *exchange a look.*

JACOB   Did you know about this?

ABIGAIL   I did not.

HEATHER   I remember days you would come to campus. Just to say hi, or drop off lunch, or bring flowers . . . I used to think about what it would be like to date a guy like you.

Awkwardness. HEATHER *looks at* JACOB; *the look is loaded. But she is the first to break it off.*

I'm sorry. That was a crazy thing to say.

ABIGAIL   Don't worry about it. We were— I was thinking about something else, is all. I got distracted.

What happens now? All three take a sip. Such a silence.

ABIGAIL *looks at* JACOB, *a little pleading. He moves to sit beside her. Takes her hand. She prompts him with a look.*

JACOB   . . . Heather.

HEATHER   Yeah.

JACOB   You're a fine editor, Abby tells me.

HEATHER   Well, that's a bit of a flattery.

JACOB   Congrats.

HEATHER   Thanks.

Susanna Florence as Heather, April Fossen as Abigail, Mark Fossen as Jacob.
Plan-B Theatre. © 2015 Rick Pollock.

JACOB   Yes. Well.

ABIGAIL   Well.

HEATHER   . . . Well?

JACOB *looks to* ABIGAIL.

ABIGAIL   Um. Well. We're so glad you're here. We have
something to—ask you.

HEATHER   Really.

ABIGAIL   Yes.

HEATHER   Okay.

ABIGAIL   We—Jacob and I—we've been asked to a part
of something potentially—

JACOB   Unprecedented?

ABIGAIL   Oh, there's precedent.

HEATHER   Now I'm intrigued.

ABIGAIL   *(to* JACOB*)* Do you want to—?

JACOB   You're doing just fine.

ABIGAIL   But shouldn't you— Shouldn't it be you? Who asks?

JACOB   It's coming from both of us. I think it has to.

ABIGAIL   *(to* HEATHER*)* What would you think about coming back to Salt Lake? Permanently?

HEATHER   I'm pretty sure I would loathe it.

JACOB   Not exactly what we were hoping for.

ABIGAIL   It could wait. Until after your trip. After Switzerland. When you're ready.

JACOB   We'd want you to be ready.

HEATHER   What exactly— You said "hoping for." And you're both so on edge. What's going on?

ABIGAIL   A really awkward question, and a peculiar request. Margaret Atwood would probably love to write about it.

HEATHER   Not like I haven't already scored points in the awkward department.

JACOB   Well, there's the baby thing.

ABIGAIL   We've been thinking about how to— About other things to try.

JACOB   And we've tried. We've tried so many. I worry that we—

ABIGAIL *shoots him a look.*

I can't help it. I worry about hurting you. How much experimenting can a body take?

ABIGAIL   *(to* HEATHER*)* I bruise easily.

HEATHER   I'll do it.

ABIGAIL   You will?

HEATHER   You want to have a baby. And you need a surrogate. I can do that. I think I can, anyway.

ABIGAIL   No— I mean, thank you, but—

JACOB   I didn't even think— Wow.

HEATHER   Isn't that what you want?

ABIGAIL   Not exactly.

JACOB   It's very thoughtful.

ABIGAIL   Yes. Incredibly sweet. But nine months—*(To* JACOB*:)* I don't know if I can say it.

JACOB   Of course you can.

HEATHER   Moving back to Salt Lake, though. That's another thing altogether.

ABIGAIL   Heather, I'm asking— We're asking—for something considerably more.

HEATHER   ... ...More?

ABIGAIL   We've been asked— Jacob and I have been called to be part of a new program in the Church. We want you to do it with us. I guess— What we're asking is if you'd be interested—willing, I suppose—to, um, marry us. Him. But it would also be me.

HEATHER *is at a loss.*

ABIGAIL   We don't need an answer now.

JACOB   You can think about it.

ABIGAIL   We would rather you thought about it.

JACOB   Of course. Take your time.

HEATHER   You're saying— What you're saying— It's not possible.

She laughs; she can't help it.

I just— You're asking me to marry you? Both of you? That's nuts.

ABIGAIL   It is what it is.

HEATHER   . . . So this is happening.

ABIGAIL   Pretty much.

HEATHER   *(to* JACOB*)* And you're all right with this? I'm assuming they asked you first.

JACOB   They asked us together. We decided together.

HEATHER   You decided together. That must be nice.

JACOB: We thought—

HEATHER   You thought I was desperate. Lonely.

ABIGAIL   No—

HEATHER   What makes you think I want to be your second wife? Anyone's second wife?

ABIGAIL   I thought it would be better to ask someone I knew. Someone I already loved and admired.

HEATHER   You admire me?

ABIGAIL   Of course I do. You have ambition. Drive. You're a force to be reckoned with. It's only a matter of time before you have a book contract of your own.

HEATHER   He's your husband.

ABIGAIL   I'm not giving him to you.

HEATHER   Then what are you doing?

ABIGAIL   Sharing. Him.

JACOB   Still in the room.

HEATHER   How does this work exactly? I'll tell you, I was the kid on the playground who didn't want to take turns on the swings. I'd run out of class first to claim mine, and then I wouldn't give it up, all recess long, until someone pulled me out of it. I suck at sharing.

ABIGAIL   I don't know. I guess that's what we have to figure out.

HEATHER   What do you mean, you don't know?

ABIGAIL   I mean, I don't know.

HEATHER   You're asking me to— How can you not have a plan?

ABIGAIL   This is all new to me too. All right? We all know what the ideal would be, and that this is not it. I thought, What can I do to make this situation more tolerable?

HEATHER   And the answer was to call me.

ABIGAIL   I can't explain it. But yes.

JACOB   Look. We know how crazy this all sounds. I don't know that we've completely come to grips with it ourselves. But you're the closest thing Abby has to family. Her students are her children.

HEATHER   … I used to wish you were my sister. I looked for excuses to visit you in your office almost every day. Coming here was like—

Are you saying this is my only chance? To get married?

ABIGAIL   Of course not.

HEATHER   I wanted it a long time ago, when I was an undergrad and a fairy tale wedding was what everyone wanted. But finishing BYU single was liberating in a way. I didn't need to get married to be whole. I was— I am me. I have a job. I support myself. I go to church on Sunday and I think how blessed I am to be in complete control of my life. To only have to worry about what I want. Sometimes, though, there is that little nagging feeling that something—someone is missing. I'll come home late from work, and my apartment is dark and quiet. Most days, I relish the quiet. But now and then I can't help but wonder what those floors would sound like with more than one person walking across them. I sit on the couch and pull a blanket around myself and wish I could be—held.

ABIGAIL   Honey—

HEATHER   It's nothing new. I'm fine. Marriage is not part of my plan right now. It hasn't been for a while. I'm thirty-three. So what? There's nothing wrong with being single at thirty-three.

JACOB   No. Of course not.

ABIGAIL   This was a bad idea. I'm sorry. I shouldn't have presumed. I was being selfish. I didn't think— I didn't mean to insult you.

JACOB   Not at all. We were trying to figure out who would—work best with us. Abby thought of you first.

ABIGAIL   I miss you. I miss our talks. I thought that if we were crazy enough to do this thing, Jacob and I, then you were the natural choice to do it with us. The thought just came into my head, an item to check off on a to-do list. Like it was ordinary. Expected.

HEATHER   "Kindred spirits." That's what you used to call us.

ABIGAIL   Yes. I still believe it.

HEATHER   It's always been a comfort to me.

Silence.

I should go.

But she stops. Her expression is thoughtful.

ABIGAIL   You're exhausted, I'm sure. Where are you staying? We have a spare room upstairs. I should have told you that in the first place.

JACOB   We'll pay for the room.

HEATHER   . . . Abby . . .

ABIGAIL looks up at her tone.

Abby, I— What happens if I say yes?

ABIGAIL   Are you— Did you—feel something? Just now?

HEATHER sucks in a breath. She is blinking back tears. Somehow she manages to nod. ABIGAIL takes HEATHER'S hand in both of hers.

Okay, then. Okay.

Still holding hands, they sit on the couch together.

HEATHER   . . . . . . Wow. Can we, I don't know— Go to dinner or something? Catch a movie, maybe? Are there rules? For dating?

ABIGAIL   I guess we make them up.

HEATHER and JACOB exit. ABIGAIL blogs.

And that's what we did. We made up the rules as we went. We three—dated. Heather returned to San Francisco on the red-eye Sunday night, but came out to see us every other weekend. Dinners, movies, musicals at the West Valley Hale. Oh, I hate musicals. Jake acted in them in school—he's been Tony in *West Side Story* like three times— so he loves to go. One year for Christmas he gave me season tickets to the Hale and I think he was a little devastated that I didn't shriek in delight. Heather, though, apparently knows all the words to *You're a Good Man, Charlie Brown*. Who knew?

My husband and I were dating, and not necessarily each other. I don't know which of us was the third wheel; it was like we were taking turns. I mean, how does this work? Really? How did the early saints do this? How did it not hurt? No, it had to have hurt. It had to have changed everything.

Late at night after Jake had gone to bed, I would sit up watching episodes of *Sister Wives* and *Big Love*. Still none of this made the slightest bit of sense to me. I don't think it does until you find yourself living it.

There was one night when I had a pile of grading I couldn't escape. I sent them out on their own, and to be by myself . . . Well, it was edging on blissful. As for the two of them . . .

She exits. Lights shift our attention to JACOB *and* HEATHER, *on a walk downtown. Silence.*

JACOB   . . . So.

HEATHER   So. I feel like we've had this conversation before.

JACOB   Do you?

HEATHER   It's just strange. I mean— I don't know what I mean. We could just—

JACOB   Get to know each other. Without Abby filling in the blanks.

HEATHER   Exactly.

Silence. Eye contact. Shy smiles on both sides.

You can start. I don't mind.

JACOB   I'm sorry. I'm out of practice. I haven't done this since— Well, since Abby.

HEATHER   You haven't gone to dinner with someone you don't really know?

JACOB   Not in this context, no. I was never good at dating.

HEATHER   I didn't do a lot of it myself.

JACOB   Really?

HEATHER   You're surprised.

JACOB   You're so confident. Secure in yourself, in your talent. In what you're supposed to do.

HEATHER   Well, I was. Until this. I did not expect this.

JACOB   Who does? But really. Did you choose not to date?

HEATHER   I wouldn't say that, no. It just didn't happen. I was taught growing up that the guys do the asking. That you wait for them to ask. And they didn't.

JACOB   Because they're all toolboxes.

HEATHER   Well, there is that. I've been told many a time that I'm a better friend than I am a girlfriend. Apparently I'm intimidating.

JACOB   Huh.

HEATHER   Right?

JACOB   I just can't imagine— If I were an undergrad and I had you in a class—

HEATHER   Physical Science 100?

JACOB   If I had a class with you, I'd find a reason to go.

HEATHER   You're not the first married man to tell me that.

. . . So, so, SO awkward . . .

I just killed it, didn't I? We were building a rapport and I killed it. Hacked it to death with a machete. I'm sorry.

JACOB   Don't be. We're both new at this. New-ish. But I have to ask: Have a lot of married men asked you out?

HEATHER   Not for the same reason you are. But yes. Quite a few.

JACOB   So the single guys pass, but the married guys—

HEATHER   Knocking down my door.

JACOB   Wow. I feel like I should apologize.

HEATHER   There was one guy who, shall we say, wasn't intimidated.

JACOB   Single or married?

HEATHER   Very single. It may be hard to believe, but I didn't ever actually go out with someone else's husband. Until . . .

JACOB   You said you didn't date.

HEATHER   I don't count Adam. I don't know why. We were so comfortable together that we didn't date. We were just—together. Either at his place or mine. We didn't go out. We cooked, we studied, we watched '80s movies on a VHS player he bought at a yard sale.

JACOB   Where'd you get the tapes?

HEATHER   The public library had an amazing selection. Random foreign films. Whole seasons of BBC sitcoms. And the classics, like *Ladyhawke*. All on VHS, and all for free.

JACOB   Nice.

HEATHER   We didn't do the dance, if you know what I mean. We just—were us.

JACOB   Until?

HEATHER   Until he proposed. It was all wrong. I mean, Adam pretty much asked me to marry him because his mother told him to. He was the only kid in his family not married, and she was worried about him being single for too long. Being

Susanna Florence as Heather, Mark Fossen as Jacob, Plan-B Theatre. © 2015 Rick Pollock.

alone. She collected brides for her boys like my grandmother collected spoons. But satisfying his mother wasn't a good enough reason for me. Even though his dad kept telling me I was "a real catch." I wouldn't be lying if I said it felt sometimes like his parents were more interested in me than he was. What about you?

JACOB **Me?**

HEATHER Tell me about you. You and Abby.

JACOB It's always been about Abby.

HEATHER And . . .?

He smiles at the memory.

JACOB She didn't drive before we moved west. She grew up on the East Coast, you know that. No need for a car. It was different in the Midwest, where the buses were infrequent and stopped running after ten. I taught her how to drive, late at night, in the Hancher parking lot. I had my dad's old Audi at the time, a 5-speed that constantly smelled of gas. But man, it handled great. I used to rip up the canyon in that bad boy like—

He stops himself.

HEATHER Like?

JACOB It doesn't matter.

HEATHER Of course it does.

JACOB It's just— Driving is one of the few things I do by myself. Abby gets motion sickness. She's never been physically strong. You know? She pretty much hates driving. That's probably the real reason she never got her license until she had to.

HEATHER I love long drives.

JACOB   That Audi looked like a mess but felt like a coupe. It just hugged the road, you know? I'd forget how fast I was going. I got pulled over more than once.

HEATHER   How fast were you going?

JACOB   Got caught going 106 once. This was years later. It was late on a Sunday night, and the freeway was practically empty. It was a $400 ticket. Yeah, that was not a good night. Abby had had her third miscarriage that day. She was the most despondent I'd ever seen her. No. She wasn't even despondent. She was—still. Utterly quiet. She wouldn't talk to me, and it was like— I couldn't win her back from wherever she was. We came home from the hospital and she just went to bed. I couldn't sleep. I was all nerves and raw anger. So I went speeding west on I-80 like I was playing Mario Kart. I think that cop, pulling me over, probably saved my life.

HEATHER   Because he stopped you.

JACOB   Something like that. Anyway. I have distinct memories of trying to talk Grad School Abby through shifting gears—you couldn't really talk Grad School Abby into much of anything—and the Audi ka-chunk-ka-chunk-ka-chunking all around the parking lot. She was learning it, but more slowly than she liked, and she got frustrated. I borrowed my roommate's Prizm to teach her after that. Automatic everything.

HEATHER   We could go for a drive sometime.

JACOB   Sure. I mean, if you want.

HEATHER   If you want. Depends on one thing.

JACOB   What's that?

HEATHER   What do you listen to when you're going all bad boy up Big Cottonwood Canyon?

JACOB   *(automatic)* Radiohead. Some Chili Peppers, some Smashing Pumpkins. But Radiohead . . .

HEATHER   "Exit Music." Or "Fake—"

JACOB   *(overlapping)* "Fake Plastic Trees." That's the good stuff.

HEATHER   Yeah. It really is.

The lights shift back to ABIGAIL *and her book. She looks up at the sound of the door.*

HEATHER *and* JACOB *enter, cracking each other up.*

JACOB   I don't believe you.

HEATHER   I swear, that's exactly what happened. This cat got stuck in the gutter above the garage roof. He was meowing like crazy; you'd think he was soloing at the Met. So we got out the ladder and we argued who was going to get him down. Finally I just climbed the ladder and I reached for this cat and he swatted at me. Scratched my eye and my temple. It bled like nobody's business. I still have the scar.

She leans in to show him her temple; they stand very close.

JACOB   Yeah . . . Look at that. He got you in the eye?

She looks up at him, and they don't move away from each other.

ABIGAIL   That was the night I thought it was going to work. And I knew I didn't want it to.

She looks at the book in her hand.

I discovered the healing power of the written word when I was in junior high. I had begged my parents to let me go with my friends to a concert. New Kids on the Block were on their Magic Summer Tour. My parents said no, who knows why. I thought the world would end that night. I was sure I was going to curl up and die of a broken heart. I bawled my eyes out until I realized no one was coming upstairs in a miraculous change of attitude, and I sulked until I got bored. Then I pulled down a book. *Little Women.*

There's a bookmark in the spot.

I was morbid at thirteen; suicide was a distant, romantic possibility, and the mark of a good story was a good death scene. *Little Women* was no exception. I opened it right to "Chapter Forty: The Valley of the Shadow." Spoiler alert: Beth dies. I knew it already. I knew the book backward and forward; we were old friends. But reading about Beth's death that night, that night when I thought the whole world was against my 13-year-old self, was a comfort. Someone, even a fictional someone in a book, was having a worse day than I was. And suddenly I could deal. It's an old trick, probably more than a little silly. But you know, it still works.

Heather and Jacob were married on a Friday in August. We were married? I don't know the right thing to say. Either way, we were all sealed in the Bountiful Temple. It was an odd day. The sealing room was warm. There was a fly buzzing high, near the vaulted ceiling. I was dressed nicely—like I would be for anyone's wedding. I sat there like I was a friend, or an aunt, or a sister. Listening to the ceremony, it made no mention of me or the fact that Jacob was in fact already married. I wondered if deceased women ever witnessed their husbands remarrying, and how it made them feel. In that moment I felt separated from myself. From what was happening. Displaced somehow. I saw myself kneeling across the altar from Jacob, just as I had fourteen years before. Holding his hand and fighting the urge to push his hair out of his eyes. The memory was so fresh. Was that moment, our moment, somehow nullified or lessened by this one?

That first night—Jacob and Heather's wedding night—there was no reception. The three of us came home together. And everything was different.

Lights shift as the HUSTENS *come home—all three of them.* JACOB *carries a suitcase.*

JACOB   Welcome home. Everyone.

HEATHER   Thanks? I think. Such a strange feeling.

ABIGAIL   Indeed. Hello and welcome to the deep end.

JACOB   I'll just put this in your room.

He takes the suitcase off.

HEATHER   Well.

ABIGAIL   Well. Here we are.

HEATHER   Just like that. Instant family.

ABIGAIL   I always knew we were meant to be sisters. I'm so glad it's you.

HEATHER *hugs her.*

JACOB   *(coming in)* Hey, Abby, where are the— Oh. Sorry.

ABIGAIL   It's okay. I'm done. I'm good.

HEATHER   Look. I know this all upside down and inside out and whatever. I don't want to get in the way or disrupt your routines. This is going to take some adjustment. Some getting used to. I get that. All I know is I don't want to be the third wheel.

ABIGAIL   You're not. You won't be.

JACOB   I'm not going to lie. I'm going to have work on it.

HEATHER   That's all you can do. All I can ask.

She exits. JACOB *watches her go. Silence.*

JACOB   Oh, Abby. Abby, I don't know . . . This is so weird. It's crazy. She's in our house.

ABIGAIL   She's your wife.

JACOB   So are you.

ABIGAIL   The Lord wants you to do this.

JACOB: You're only saying that to make yourself feel better.

ABIGAIL   It's not exactly working.

JACOB   I've never wanted to be with anyone but you.

ABIGAIL   You're lying. There must have been days. I know there've been days when you've passed someone like her on the street and breathed in a heady, unfamiliar scent that clung to you for hours afterward. You smelled it again and again, wondering if you wouldn't be better off. If you'd never asked me. If you didn't get stuck.

JACOB   You don't get to say what I regret. You sure like guessing at it though. I don't know why.

ABIGAIL   Like it? What is there to like? I don't want to think about you thinking about someone else. That's just—

JACOB   And suddenly the best way to solve that problem is to bring another someone home to stay.

ABIGAIL   It's all right. I don't mind.

JACOB: Now who's lying?

ABIGAIL   She's waiting.

JACOB   Let her wait.

ABIGAIL   Jacob.

JACOB   What if I'm not ready? Can't I take a minute?

ABIGAIL   And you didn't have that thought six hours ago?

JACOB   We should have never agreed to this. Never gone this far. What are we doing here?

ABIGAIL   What we are asked to.

JACOB   Don't bring this back to faith.

ABIGAIL   What is it if it's not faith?

JACOB   Are you going to stand there and tell me you're going to tell me to have sex with another woman just because—

ABIGAIL   Not just another woman. Your wife.

JACOB   I can't, Abby.

ABIGAIL   You can. You will. This is the way our family is supposed to grow. If it helps you to think of me—

JACOB   Will you forgive me?

ABIGAIL   There's nothing to forgive. I promise.

JACOB   Just say it.

ABIGAIL   Say it?

JACOB   Forgive me.

ABIGAIL   Jake—

JACOB   I know they're just words. I know you can string them together without thinking. I just need to hear you say it.

ABIGAIL   Fine. I forgive you.

She knows it sounds wrong. Too fast. Wrong. She tries again.

Jacob. I forgive you.

JACOB Thank you.

ABIGAIL I have an idea. *(She calls:)* Heather!

Take her downtown. Get a room at the Grand America. It's a honeymoon. She deserves a honeymoon.

JACOB Abby—

ABIGAIL Go. Please.

HEATHER *(entering)* What's going on?

ABIGAIL Don't unpack anything. You're going out.

HEATHER You're not—?

ABIGAIL I'm most assuredly not. Get your bag. Jake, go grab a couple things. I'm not changing my mind. You're going.

JACOB I'm not leaving you behind.

ABIGAIL I'm not behind. I'm here. I'm fine. You should go.

Finally he nods and exits, HEATHER *following.*

The light pulls tight around ABIGAIL. *She fights to keep it together.*

ABIGAIL That night, I realized the kitchen faucet was dripping. Subtly. Slowly. I think I only noticed it because I happened to be staring at it. Over the course of about fifteen seconds, a thin lunette of water would form along the inside edge of the spout, steadily thickening. Rounding until its weight was too much and it fell with a nearly imperceptible "plop" against the steel basin. I imagine if the faucet were sentient, if it were struggling to hold each droplet back—straining with all its might, almost managing to haul that burden—that single glimmering bead—back where it belongs. But the water is a force; it wants to move, it wants to go, and there is no holding it. Suddenly it's gone, dashed and invisible, another ready to take its place.

I was mesmerized. I leaned against the granite countertop and watched drop after drop. I reached out to catch a drop with a finger, raising my hand so that it ran down my arm to my elbow, a tiny shiver of cold. A matching shiver went down my spine.

Father, is this thy plan?

There was no answer. Not in that moment. Nothing but the memory of a blossom of warmth in my heart, and a sparkle of cold on my fingertips. I wiped my hand on a towel and left the kitchen. I probably should have taken a notebook and a pen upstairs. But I took a collection of Alice Munro's short fiction instead and went to bed.

That first Sunday, none of us knew what to expect. We were fine strolling toward church. The movement was comforting; we easily fell into a rhythm.

But once we rounded the final corner and stepped onto the asphalt of the chapel parking lot, everything stopped. I don't know that we were worried or afraid. It was just a strange sensation. We were— we are—a family. We stood there together, looking at the meeting house door like it would burst into flames. But it didn't. Jacob reached for my left hand with his right; on his left, Heather put her arm through his. I couldn't tell you why— I was in a bit of a daze—but I took that first step toward the main door, and Jacob and Heather followed. There was no arguing, no hesitation. We fell into step and walked in together, a united front: a triptych of plural love and uncertainty.

There were eyes on us, I'm sure. The quiet was amazing. Everyone was probably fighting the urge to whisper. Even the children, who are normally whooping before the opening hymn, were hushed somehow. We sat in our usual pew, the only difference being that, because of Heather, I was nearer the wall than I was used to.

I don't remember much of the meeting. I was clutching Jacob's hand. He didn't react; just let me squeeze the life out of his fingers. I'm not sure if he had much feeling in either arm, as he was probably being squeezed on the other side as well. Is this what it's like to be a celebrity? If it is, I'm fairly certain I don't like it.

JACOB Are you going to do it?

ABIGAIL Not alone.

HEATHER We could all go together.

ABIGAIL   There is no going. They'll send a camera crew here and do a live feed. But we don't want to do that.

HEATHER   It's *The Today Show*.

ABIGAIL   I've always wanted to be on *The Today Show*. But I always thought it would be for my work.

JACOB   If you don't want to . . .

ABIGAIL   Do you think they want us to? The Brethren?

JACOB   They may just be more done with secrets than we give them credit for.

The three sit together on the couch, JACOB *in the center, smiling at the unseen camera crew.*

HEATHER   Well, there's a lot of compromise. A lot of— sharing. I'm a creature of habit, and I came into this situation used to being on my own. I'm good at being selfish, I guess.

JACOB   We all are, I think. There are things you don't take issue with sharing because you've never considered the possibility. Time, for one thing. There's never enough.

ABIGAIL   It's pretty much what I imagined. Different. Difficult. Jacob has his own room now; we each do, and we split our time. I try to think about it in very simple terms—very straightforward. Almost clinical, if that makes sense. Days on a calendar, marks on a page. I go through the motions because doing more than that will sting.

Lights shift, and the live taping is over. All three fall back into the couch in relief.

HEATHER   To think I used to want to be Jennifer Lawrence.

JACOB   Take comfort in the fact that Jennifer Lawrence might just see you on television.

ABIGAIL   I got an email this morning. From Hulu.

JACOB   What?

HEATHER   Why?

ABIGAIL   A reality show. They want to follow us around for a year.

JACOB   Oh, gosh. Thank goodness they contacted you.

ABIGAIL   Why do you say that?

JACOB   Because you're the most likely to say no.

ABIGAIL   Would you have said yes?

JACOB   No. *(Indicating* HEATHER*)* She would have.

HEATHER   Is that a bad thing?

ABIGAIL   Well—

JACOB   You did, didn't you? You said no?

ABIGAIL   I did.

JACOB   *(overlapping)* Oh, good.

HEATHER   *(overlapping)* But you can call them back.

ABIGAIL   No.

HEATHER   There's probably a lot of money attached to it. We could quit working—

ABIGAIL   Quit working and live in a bubble. No thanks.

HEATHER   Yeah, well. We're already in a bubble. We might as well get paid for it.

She exits. ABIGAIL *and* JACOB *sit so for a moment. He looks at her. She doesn't move, doesn't look back at him.*

Under the following, HEATHER *reappears on the edge of the light.*

ABIGAIL   "Now Sarai Abram's wife bare him no children: and she had a handmaiden, an Egyptian, whose name was Hagar.

"And Sarai said unto Abram, Behold now, the Lord hath restrained me from bearing: I pray thee, go in unto my maid; it may be that I may obtain children by her. And Abram hearkened to the voice of Sarai.

"And Sarai Abram's wife took Hagar her maid the Egyptian and gave her to her husband Abram to be his wife.

"And he went into Hagar, and she conceived."

JACOB *goes to* HEATHER. *She takes him by the hand and they exit together.*

I've always said Jake was the good sort. It was a phrase of my father's. When Jake and I started dating seriously, I took him home to meet my parents. It was Thanksgiving, and we got dumped on: almost two feet of snow overnight. In the morning, I found Daddy on the porch watching

Jake shovel the drive. "He beat me to it," Dad said. "I didn't even have to ask him." He tuned to look at me and said, "This fellow, he's the good sort." It just stuck with me.

Dad was right. There have been so many mornings when I haven't wanted to even get out of bed, knowing that day would just be a crap-fest. But Jake has always been there, showing me he cared in some little way. Since Heather came into our lives, I can't help but feel the weight of separation. Knowing he's not with me at the same time that he's down the hall is one of the most harrowing thoughts I'll ever have. But he still finds ways to surprise me.

Lights shift to another day. The family all lounge in the living room. HEATHER *is several months pregnant.*

Have you thought at all about names?

JACOB   Not a lot.

HEATHER   Jake refuses to let the baby be a junior.

JACOB   Someday he'll be a junior in high school. Hopefully college. But no, he will not be Jacob Junior. It'll melt and fade into J. J.

HEATHER   And we can't have that.

JACOB   No. We can't.

HEATHER   I was thinking about Thomas.

ABIGAIL   Is it a family name?

HEATHER   My favorite uncle. He was always there even when my dad wasn't.

JACOB   I like it.

HEATHER   If we go with Thomas, you should choose his middle name.

JACOB   All right. Scott.

ABIGAIL stops. Looks at him.

ABIGAIL   Just like that?

JACOB   Of course.

HEATHER   Thomas Scott Husten. I'm a fan.

ABIGAIL   Me too.

HEATHER   Where's it from? The Scott?

JACOB   It's Abby's maiden name.

HEATHER and JACOB exit as the lights shift.

It's late. ABIGAIL is alone in the living room, writing. Revising. Concentrating. Somewhere an infant cries. ABIGAIL looks up at the sound.

HEATHER   *(from off)* Jake? Could you? Please?

JACOB   *(from off)* Coming, I'm coming . . .

He appears in the doorway, the baby in his arms. ABIGAIL is there to meet him.

JACOB   Abby?

Mark Fossen as Jacob, April Fossen as Abigail, Susanna Florence as Heather.
Plan-B Theatre. © 2015 Rick Pollock.

She takes the child from him, giving him a book in exchange.

ABIGAIL   Don't worry, I'll take care of him. I'm already up.

JACOB   But you're working.

ABIGAIL   It's fine.

JACOB   Are you sure?

ABIGAIL   Yeah. Go to sleep.

JACOB exits. ABIGAIL rocks the baby, humming softly. The crying fades to nothing.

I never knew . . . I thought it would be different. I thought I would make some kind of break. He would be theirs, and Jake and I would go back to being Jake and I. Jake and me? Us. But you can't draw arbitrary lines in a shared space. You can only go so long before you run into each other. Normal is good, normal is the goal. And then there was this little guy . . . This little, squinty-faced, green-eyed, bald guy who can scream to bring avalanches down the Pyrenees. *(To the baby:)* Such a crotchety old man. We're going to be best friends.

Lights shift to a new day around ABIGAIL; *she continues to hold the baby when* JACOB *comes in, just about ready for work.*

JACOB Hey.

ABIGAIL Hey.

He kisses her cheek. She looks at him, but he's looking at the child.

JACOB Looking good, little man.

HEATHER *enters, also dressed for work. She's a bit harried. Perhaps snappish.*

HEATHER Morning.

JACOB Morning.

Their turn for a kiss.

HEATHER   Abby, can you take him this morning? I have
       to drive down to Provo for a meeting.

ABIGAIL   All right.

JACOB   It's not a problem?

ABIGAIL   It's not a problem.

HEATHER   Thank you so much. C'mon, Jake, I'll drop
       you at the train.

JACOB   Bye, Ab.

They are gone, and there is beautiful quiet.

ABIGAIL   It was never a problem. I went on sabbatical
       to finish the book. I'd forgotten how nice it was
       to work at home. Sometimes I think I should miss
       teaching. But it's become one of those distant
       fuzzy things I'm glad I've done and I'm okay not
       doing anymore.

*Gently she places the sleeping Thomas in the crev-
ice of the couch cushions. Taking up her pen and
notes, she works.*

*Lights fade to another evening. After a bit, the baby
cries.*

HEATHER *enters and picks up the baby. Rocks him.
Comforts him. He continues to cry.* HEATHER *is frustrated.*

ABIGAIL   Here, let me—

HEATHER   He's not your son.

Abby, I'm sorry. I didn't mean—

ABIGAIL   **Never mind.**

She walks away, the light following her to a second space. We can still see HEATHER, *though only faintly.*

She's right. He's not mine. But if he were . . . What am I doing here? Watching them, together, it's almost like watching home movies of my marriage, but of scenes I don't remember. I guess this means I know who the third wheel is. And maybe I don't mind nearly as much as I thought I would.

She covers her eyes. Prays.

Father, I'm exhausted. I don't know if I'm built for this. I suppose that's the point—to take what you can take and no more. But I swear this is too much . . . I think of the way he looks at her . . . The way she looks at him . . . And it hurts to breathe. I have to fight not to gasp aloud, to give a sign that this—just—hurts. Why does this have to happen?

But that's the reason. That's what faith is. Dealing with the fact that you never know enough.

She goes out. Lights shift to a new day, mid-afternoon.

HEATHER and JACOB enter together, holding hands. It doesn't take them long to get comfortable.

HEATHER   It might be kind of fun. You know, a road trip? Up the Oregon coast.

JACOB   All three of us?

HEATHER   And Thomas.

JACOB   You don't think people would get the wrong idea?

HEATHER   What idea could they possibly get that's wonkier than the truth?

JACOB   Why do we need to go anywhere?

HEATHER   Because there are so many anywheres to visit. Don't you think?

JACOB   I guess.

HEATHER   I know! The Alps. You owe me a month in Switzerland.

JACOB   What have they got that we don't?

HEATHER   The Alps. Chocolate. Lederhosen.

JACOB   I think my vote is for home.

HEATHER   Don't you want to see places you've never been? Go mountain climbing or skydiving or geo-caching.

JACOB   Geo-what?

HEATHER   Never mind.

JACOB   I guess I've never really had much of a mind for travel.

HEATHER   It's all right. Though I can think of a way you can make it up to me.

ABIGAIL *enters through the front door, excited, if a bit harried. She carries two bound galleys in the crook of one arm, her cell phone in the other hand.*

ABIGAIL   *(on the phone)* Uh huh . . . Yeah . . . So far I think they look great. I know, I know, I should let someone else handle the proofing. But I just love looking at it. It makes me giddy—

She comes into the living room and stops short.

JACOB *and* HEATHER *are kissing on the couch.*

ABIGAIL   . . . Ah. I'll call you back.

JACOB   Abby—

ABIGAIL   Don't "Abby" me. I just— I was having a good day. But now I need to rinse out my eyes with bleach.

JACOB   That's not fair.

ABIGAIL   Rules, Brother Husten. There are rules for this kind of thing. Not in public spaces.

HEATHER   It's three o'clock in the—

ABIGAIL   I'm on sabbatical, remember? Of the three of us, I'm the one that is supposed to be here right now. Care to answer that one?

HEATHER *looks up at* JACOB. *He moves to sit beside her. Together they are guilty teenagers who have been caught behind the bleachers.*

HEATHER   We met for lunch and decided to come home early.

ABIGAIL   You're skipping work to make out? What are you, fourteen?

HEATHER   The word I like is spontaneous.

ABIGAIL   You would. *(Indicating* JACOB*)* And this one hasn't been spontaneous since cub scouts, and even then it was someone else's idea.

JACOB   There's nothing wrong with having a little fun.

ABIGAIL   Right. Fun.

JACOB   Don't be mad.

ABIGAIL   I'm not— There are things you can't un-see. Whatever the two of you do in the privacy of your Thursday nights is completely up to you. I don't want to know about it.

She drops the manuscripts on a chair and exits.

Silence.

HEATHER glances at JACOB. *After a bit she begins to giggle.* JACOB *half-smiles, but he's uncomfortable.* HEATHER *bursts out laughing.*

JACOB   Such a troublemaker.

HEATHER reaches for a manuscript.

What is it?

HEATHER   Galleys. For her book.

Lights shift to ABIGAIL'S *blogosphere.*

ABIGAIL   I wish she were my student now so I could fail her. Rules, you know. Very simple rules. The calendar, to make sure things are evenly split. Wednesdays and Saturdays for her, Tuesdays and Fridays for me. Mondays are family night. Pretty simple and straightforward until—

HEATHER   Can I trade you next Saturday night for Friday the 25th?

ABIGAIL   Really? Is this what my life is right now?

I find solace in, of all things, grocery shopping. The gentle metallic whirring of the cart's wheels, the low jazz covers of Beyoncé, the aisles filled with bright and inviting packages. The clearance aisle is almost always filled with marvelous things. Seconds and rejects and leftovers, marked down to fifty and sometimes seventy-five percent off. There are always treasures to be found there, oftentimes the ones you least expect. Most of the time it's just the packaging that's damaged—a dented box of cupcakes, for example. The cupcakes haven't been touched, and they're individually wrapped, but no one will buy the broken box at full price. Because really, everyone buys cupcakes for the box, right? Pristine and perfect, with sharp corners and straight edges, just waiting for someone to tear into it. We like things to look new. Never mind the disturbing fact that those cupcakes are brimming with preservatives that might just keep them looking new into the next millennium.

Susanna Florence as Heather and April Fossen as Abigail. Plan-B Theatre. © 2015 Rick Pollock.

Damaged goods. Are the stewed tomatoes in a dented can really going to taste different than the ones in a normal can? No. But the dented cans end up in the clearance aisle, because somehow they are, in someone's mind, imperfect.

We came to this earth to be imperfect. To be mortal and malleable. Human. That was the point. So why do we torment ourselves with perfect expectations none of us can attain? Happiness isn't perfection; it's realizing that you aren't perfect and accepting that you may never be. And that is just fine.

Lights shift to a new day—an average day. ABIGAIL *does the Sunday crossword.* HEATHER *reads nearby.*

ABIGAIL   "Main thoroughfare." Six letters.

HEATHER   Six? Freeway is too many, highway is too many. What do you have so far?

ABIGAIL   Ends in a "y."

HEATHER *takes the newspaper.*

HEATHER   Six letters for a thoroughfare. Not street.
Ah! Artery.

ABIGAIL   Nice.

HEATHER   Here's one for you. Seven letters. American
author of the coming-of-age novel *Summer*.

ABIGAIL   Wharton. It's Edith Wharton.

HEATHER   Wharton! I knew that.

HEATHER *exits. After a moment* JACOB *comes in.* ABI-
GAIL *hardly looks up at him. Continues working on
her puzzle. Silence. Finally:*

JACOB   Hey.

ABIGAIL   Hey. I think I'm going to turn in. I'll see you
in the morning.

JACOB   Abby, wait.

ABIGAIL   What?

JACOB   Don't you want to— Come sit with me.

ABIGAIL   Not now. I'm pretty tired. Thomas didn't
sleep too well last night.

JACOB   He's asleep now. Please, Abby.

They go to the couch and sit.

ABIGAIL Was there something you wanted to talk about?

JACOB No. Not necessarily. I was just thinking about your voice and how I used to hear it all the time. But now it's like—it's like you're barely here. You're so quiet.

ABIGAIL I like the quiet.

JACOB I miss you.

ABIGAIL I haven't gone anywhere.

JACOB No, but it's like you're not really here. You're checked out. Has something happened? Something I should know about?

ABIGAIL Just—days. Days melting into nights giving way to new days.

JACOB I've always liked the way you say things. Even when I don't quite follow.

ABIGAIL You follow just fine.

JACOB I spell like a tenth grader.

ABIGAIL Oh, are we talking about spelling? In that case—

JACOB Don't! Spare me, please.

A snort from ABIGAIL.

Ha! I did it. I made you laugh.

ABIGAIL Did not. That was a chuckle. *(Off his look:)* Fine, a snort. Either way it's a very different thing.

Besides, the only way you make me laugh is by being absolutely pathetic.

He looks at her for a long moment.

ABIGAIL   What?

JACOB   There you are. That's the Abby I remember. The twinkling.

ABIGAIL   I hate that word.

JACOB   I know.

ABIGAIL   "K" is a serious letter. It makes knives all sharp and stealthy. It deserves a better word than twinkling.

JACOB   Twinkling is good for the soul. Stars in the sky. We'll get some of those glow-in-the-dark ones to stick on the ceiling in Thomas's room. Twinkling will be his first Mozart.

ABIGAIL   It actually will be. The tune for "Twinkle, Twinkle, Little Star" is a variation on a French folk song, adapted by Mozart.

JACOB   Really.

ABIGAIL   Mhmm. It's the same tune as both "Baa, Baa, Black Sheep" and "The Alphabet Song."

JACOB   What would I do without you?

ABIGAIL   Be a very good father.

JACOB   I can't do that without you. There's no way. Because you're the very best of—*(He suddenly has a bad taste in his mouth).* Sister-moms?

She laughs. She can't help it.

ABIGAIL No. Please, no.

JACOB But you're going to mother him as much as we are.

ABIGAIL It's fine. The word doesn't matter. "Aunt" is fine. I'm not his mother. I'm not going to lie to him. Let's not confuse him before he can walk.

JACOB Is that the right word? "Aunt"?

ABIGAIL It is if we say it is.

JACOB Do you like it?

ABIGAIL I know I like it better than "sister-mom."

JACOB Aunt Abby. Sounds nice.

ABIGAIL Mhmm.

JACOB Are you happy?

ABIGAIL Enough.

JACOB I used to make you happy.

ABIGAIL I used to make you happy.

JACOB What changed?

ABIGAIL Nothing. Just—everything.

Sitting together, they are very comfortable; no more, no less.

A slow fade to black. End of play.

MELISSA LEILANI LARSON is a novelist turned playwright and screenwriter. Her produced plays include *The Edible Complex* (commissioned by Plan-B Theatre), *Pilot Program, Pride and Prejudice* (commissioned by Brigham Young University), *The Weaver of Raveloe, Persuasion, Little Happy Secrets, Martyrs' Crossing, A Flickering, Standing Still Standing, Lady in Waiting,* and the upcoming *Mountain Law*. Films include *Jane and Emma* and *Freetown*.

Honors include: the Ghana Movie Award for Best Screenplay; the Utah Film Award for Best Picture; three Association for Mormon Letters Drama Awards; the IRAM Best New Play award; the Mayhew Playwriting Award; a Salt Lake City Weekly Arty Award; winning the LDS Film Festival Feature Writing Competition and the Lewis National Playwriting Contest for Women; and being named an O'Neill National Playwrights Conference semi-finalist.

Mel is a proud member of the Dramatists Guild, serving as the Utah Ambassador. She is also a member of Plan-B Theatre's Lab. She holds a BA in English from BYU and an MFA from the Iowa Playwrights Workshop. Mel enjoys melty cheese, hedgehogs, puzzles, nice paper, and nicer pens.

Ⓢ

MelissaLeilaniLarson.com

🐦

@mel_leilani